OXFORD WORLD'S CLASSICS

BORIS GODUNOV

AND OTHER DRAMATIC WORKS

ALEXANDER SERGEEVICH PUSHKIN was born in Moscow in 1799 into an old aristocratic family. In 1817 he received a nominal appointment in the government service, but for the most part he led a dissipated life in the capital while he continued to produce much highly polished light verse. His narrative poem, *Ruslan and Lyudmila* (pub. 1820), brought him widespread fame. At about the same time a few mildly seditious verses led to his banishment from the capital. During this so-called 'southern exile', he composed several narrative poems and began his novel in verse, *Eugene Onegin*. As a result of further conflicts with state authorities he was condemned to a new period of exile at his family's estate of Mikhailovskoe. There he wrote some of his finest lyric poetry, completed his verse drama *Boris Godunov*, and continued work on *Eugene Onegin*. He was still in enforced absence from the capital when the Decembrist revolt of 1825 took place. Although several of his friends were among those executed or imprisoned, he was not implicated in the affair; and in 1826 he was pardoned by the new Tsar Nicholas I and permitted to return to Moscow. By the end of the decade, as he sought to become a truly professional writer, he turned increasingly to prose composition. In the especially fruitful autumn of 1830, while stranded by cholera at his estate of Boldino, he completed *Eugene Onegin*, wrote a major collection of prose stories (*The Tales of Belkin*), and composed his experimental *Little Tragedies*. In 1831 he married Natalya Goncharova and sought to put his personal and professional affairs on a more stable footing. The rest of his life, however, was plagued by financial and marital woes, by the hostility of literary and political enemies, and by the younger generation's dismissal of his recent work. His literary productivity diminished, but in the remarkable 'second Boldino autumn' of 1833 he produced both his greatest prose tale, *The Queen of Spades*, and a last poetic masterpiece, *The Bronze Horseman*. In 1836 he completed his only novel-length work in prose, *The Captain's Daughter*. Beleaguered by numerous adversaries and enraged by anonymous letters containing attacks on his honour, in 1837 he was driven to challenge an importunate admirer of his wife to a duel. The contest took place on 27 January, and two days later the poet died from his wounds.

JAMES E. FALEN is Professor Emeritus of Russian at the University of Tennessee. He is the author of *Isaac Babel: Russian Master of the Short Story* (University of Tennessee Press, 1974) and has translated Pushkin's novel in verse, *Eugene Onegin*, for Oxford World's Classics.

CARYL EMERSON is A. Watson Armour III University Professor of Slavic Languages and Literatures at Princeton University. She has published widely on Mikhail Bakhtin and on Pushkin, Dostoevsky, Tolstoy, Russian literary criticism, and Russian operatic and song repertory.

OXFORD WORLD'S CLASSICS

For over 100 years Oxford World's Classics have brought readers closer to the world's great literature. Now with over 700 titles—from the 4,000-year-old myths of Mesopotamia to the twentieth century's greatest novels—the series makes available lesser-known as well as celebrated writing.

The pocket-sized hardbacks of the early years contained introductions by Virginia Woolf, T. S. Eliot, Graham Greene, and other literary figures which enriched the experience of reading. Today the series is recognized for its fine scholarship and reliability in texts that span world literature, drama and poetry, religion, philosophy and politics. Each edition includes perceptive commentary and essential background information to meet the changing needs of readers.

OXFORD WORLD'S CLASSICS

ALEXANDER PUSHKIN

Boris Godunov
and Other Dramatic Works

Translated with Notes by
JAMES E. FALEN

With an Introduction by
CARYL EMERSON

OXFORD
UNIVERSITY PRESS

OXFORD
UNIVERSITY PRESS

Great Clarendon Street, Oxford OX2 6DP

Oxford University Press is a department of the University of Oxford.
It furthers the University's objective of excellence in research, scholarship,
and education by publishing worldwide in

Oxford New York

Auckland Cape Town Dar es Salaam Hong Kong Karachi
Kuala Lumpur Madrid Melbourne Mexico City Nairobi
New Delhi Shanghai Taipei Toronto

With offices in

Argentina Austria Brazil Chile Czech Republic France Greece
Guatemala Hungary Italy Japan Poland Portugal Singapore
South Korea Switzerland Thailand Turkey Ukraine Vietnam

Oxford is a registered trade mark of Oxford University Press
in the UK and in certain other countries

Published in the United States
by Oxford University Press Inc., New York

Introduction © Caryl Emerson 2007
Translation and other editorial material © James E. Falen 2007

The moral rights of the authors have been asserted

Database right Oxford University Press (maker)

First published as an Oxford World's Classics paperback 2007
Reissued 2009

British Library Cataloguing in Publication Data

Data available

Library of Congress Cataloging in Publication Data

Pushkin, Aleksandr Sergeevich, 1799–1837.
[Plays. English. Selections]
Boris Godunov and other dramatic works / Alexander Pushkin ;
translated with notes by James E. Falen ; with an introduction by Caryl Emerson.
p. cm. — (Oxford world's classics (Oxford University Press))
Includes bibliographical references.
ISBN 978–0–19–955404–1 (alk. paper)
1. Pushkin, Aleksandr Sergeevich, 1799–1837—Translations into English.
I. Falen, James E., 1935–ᅠ II. Title.
PG3347.A2 2007
891.73′.3—dc22ᅠ2006028321

ISBN 978–0–19–955404–1

4

Typeset in Ehrhardt
by RefineCatch Limited, Bungay, Suffolk
Printed in Great Britain
on acid-free paper by
Clays Ltd, St Ives plc

CONTENTS

INTRODUCTION

ALEXANDER PUSHKIN (1799–1837) is Russia's most cosmopolitan playwright. This fact is sometimes obscured, because Pushkin's best-known play, *Boris Godunov* (1825), concerns Russian history, a Russian dynastic crisis, and is known outside its homeland primarily as the literary source for Modest Musorgsky's intensely nationalistic opera composed four decades later. Peel away the Kremlin gongs and ragged masses crowding the operatic stage, however, and *Boris Godunov* resonates with the most varied echoes of Western European theatre: Shakespeare, Schiller, Goethe, Corneille, Racine, Italian seriocomic opera, all of them stripped down, reduced to their essentials (as Pushkin conceived them), and presented in compact scenes that snap open and closed like entries in a medieval Russian chronicle. The four *Little Tragedies* that Pushkin wrote in 1830—so little, in fact, that they resemble the final acts of tragedies—are also stripped down and condensed. Not only are they pan-European, set respectively in a medieval castle, Vienna, Madrid, and London; they are also pan-human, each focusing on a single moral defect and its attempts to justify itself: avarice, envy, lust, and defiant feasting in the face of death. Two of the four tragedies announce their source in English playwrights. The fragmentary *Scene from Faust* builds off a German legend. *Rusalka* is a Danube River mermaid tale, shifted eastward and lightly Slavicized. In drama as elsewhere, 'Russianness' for Pushkin meant a hybrid: the ability to refract, integrate, condense, and translate everyone else.

But translation and condensation are not quite the right terms for what Pushkin does. He was cosmopolitan along a highly personal vector, and everything he touched turned irreversibly into his own trademark gold. Pushkin did not really 'borrow from' or 'translate' European poets, although in dramatic experiments he loved to start with someone else's story. He would be intrigued by another poet's choice of form, text, or narrative plot. Often he could glimpse this alien whole only partially. But what resulted was a wondrous symbiosis between Pushkin's genius—his absolute control over the lexical and rhythmic resources of the Russian language—and his linguistic 'deficiencies', a reciprocity superbly explicated by Alexander Dolinin in his discussion of 'Pushkin and English Literature'.[1] How this creative dynamic worked is crucial if we are to place the dramatic verse translated in this volume in the context Pushkin dreamed for it.

Of the European languages and cultures that stimulated Pushkin—French, English, German, and Italian—only French was deeply, thoroughly known. From early adolescence, Pushkin was utterly at home in seventeenth- and eighteenth-century French literature. But precisely because French Romantic theatre disappointed him, he resolved to look elsewhere for dramatic inspiration. He worked hard on his English beginning in 1828 (and by the early 1830s had become passively quite good with it); Italian he might have guessed at through French or absorbed through the operas of Mozart and Rossini; German he never knew. Pushkin's interest in Shakespeare, Byron, Schiller, and Goethe was mediated wherever possible through French prose translations, hearsay from friends, and French critical studies—which, Dolinin argues, liberated his genius to amend the original in his own mind and supply details out of his own personal poetics. It also permitted Pushkin to idealize second-rate poets whose simpler syntax and vocabulary he could understand (such as the now forgotten British Romantic Barry Cornwall) and to underestimate or even ignore the pontificating, verbose, and overly clever aspects of masters such as Lord Byron. Pushkin was a great cosmopolitan in the first instance because he considered himself a European and was curious about other cultures. But the limitations of his linguistic equipment shielded him from the direct aesthetic impact of the original and enabled his own genius to leak into (or even improve upon) his source. This alchemy applied to most of Pushkin's encounters with European genres between 1815 and the mid-1830s: the ode, elegy, long 'Byronic' poem, stylized folktale, neoclassical verse drama, *comédie italienne*, short story or *conte*, epistolary prose, travel notes, and eventually the prose of a historian. Dramatic form was of special urgency.

[1] Alexander Dolinin, 'Pushkin and English Literature', in David M. Bethea (ed.), *The Pushkin Handbook* (Madison, 2005), 424–57.

Pushkin adored the stage. But he was critical of most Russian performance practice in St Petersburg of his time: the pompous, stilted diction of neoclassical tragedy as well as the predictability and crudeness of most melodrama and vaudeville. Part of his alchemy was his commitment to staged spectacles that were at once fast, funny, startling, smart, and deep—whether comic or tragic. Pushkin first tried his hand at dramatic satire at the age of 16. By the mid-1820s he was not only writing a full-length play, but wished to contribute as a Russian playwright to the more general reform of European theatre. For him, being cosmopolitan meant more than just taking from other cultures. It also meant taking seriously the possibility that one could offer an innovation or synthesis of one's own that other national cultures might find useful in the evolution of their traditions.

Pushkin's fellow Russian poets were thrilled by this assumption that the Russian literary language was capable of absorbing and perhaps even adding to the European legacy. After all, England, Italy, France, and Spain had been producing masterpieces in the vernacular during those centuries when Russia, in the eyes and ears of Europeans, was savage, silent, and dark. Until the mid-eighteenth century, the written Russian language was an unwieldy mass of archaisms, awkward poetic borrowings, uncoordinated linguistic registers and mongrel styles. When compared with mature litera-tures further west, Russian was a very young and untried vehicle for secular aesthetic expression, even in Pushkin's gifted hands. But there were deeper obstacles to reciprocal, two-way cosmopolitanism. For all Pushkin's precocity and genius, 'giving back' to Europe was not easy to achieve for the brilliant aristocratic poets of his generation.

The reason was not Russian backwardness or primitiveness, but rather the reverse. Russian noblemen (and women) of letters in the empire of Nicholas I were raised at the minimum bilingually, in French and Russian. Often they commanded English or German as well. It was a rare West European who bothered to learn any Russian. And why should they? The Russian officers who occupied Paris in 1814 spoke as pure a French as any of their defeated foe. Pushkin, under police surveillance his entire adult life, was never allowed to travel outside the Russian Empire. Had he been, it would not have crossed his mind that his literary counterparts in Europe could appreciate his poems—or even decipher the alphabet in which they were printed. As far as Europe could tell, Russia in its own tongue produced little more than barbaric, visual arabesques. When Pushkin in the 1820s made an effort to enter the debates over theatre reform in the French press that had been triggered by August von Schlegel and Victor Hugo—theoretical treatises that eventually confirmed Shakespeare as the model for Romantic drama on the Continent—he knew well that his own innovative *Boris Godunov* would be accessible solely to audiences at home.[2] Nor could the spread of Pushkin's theatrical ideas happen extra-verbally, that is, through realization in a theatre and subsequent reviewing in the periodical press. Although Pushkin had hoped otherwise, no staging of his controversial historical drama took place during his lifetime. Public theatre houses in Russia had become the property of the crown in 1803 and remained an Imperial monopoly until 1882, with their repertory controlled by a government bureaucracy. If a play survived censorship for print, it was then censored for public performance, a separate and more severe filter. There were also restrictions on certain characters and themes, as in Western European theatres. No actor was allowed to depict a Romanov tsar on stage—there, Pushkin was within bounds, since his play ends eight years before the founding of the Romanov dynasty in 1613—but also forbidden were any ecclesiastics, and Pushkin's play featured several, including an irreverent Patriarch and two drunken itinerant monks. *Boris Godunov* was detained in the censor's office for six years and approved for publication only after extensive cuts and the deletion of three whole scenes. The premiere of the play (also with extensive cuts) took place only in 1870.

What might we say, then, of Pushkin as cosmopolitan dramatist? He took from everywhere, gave back to nowhere, and was never staged during his own lifetime. Whether Pushkin ever intended to create more than 'closet drama' is still debated. Most experts assume that Pushkin never intended *The Little Tragedies* for the

[2] See ch. 2, '*Boris Godunov* and the Theater', in J. Douglas Clayton, *Dimitry's Shade: A Reading of Alexander Pushkin's Boris Godunov* (Evanston, Ill., 2004), 30–53.

stage, although by the beginning of the twentieth century, each had been set as a chamber opera.[3] Sceptics point out that scene changes in Pushkin often occur with lightning speed, into and out of improbable locales. The on-stage battle scenes in *Boris* (where troops clash and horses die on stage) are not easy to envision and so brief that there is hardly time to reconnoitre. The penultimate scene of *Rusalka* takes place on the bottom of the Dnieper River. And then there is the special challenge of Pushkin's stage directions. Technically no more than acting or directing cues, inaudible and invisible to the audience, they are nevertheless always fastidiously crafted, laconic but with a narrative tone of their own. Some of Pushkin's stage directions have whole histories attached to them, most famously the final cue '*narod bezmolvstvuet*' (the people are silent/the people fall speechless) that appeared for the first time in the 1831 printed text of *Boris Godunov*. Because of its hint of moral outrage and popular resistance, it was quickly seized upon by critics as key to interpreting the entire play. (The 1825 uncensored original version of the play ended differently, with the cheer 'Long live Tsar Dimitry Ivanovich!')[4] If the 1831 variant is preferred, how should that powerful directive of non-response be performed so that it shocks an audience the way it shocks a reader? In their aborted 1937 production of *Boris Godunov*, Vsevolod Meyerhold and Sergei Prokofiev devised one solution: to introduce an untexted humming chorus, crescendo it throughout the final scenes, and then, at the last moment, abruptly cut it off. Like a pistol shot, the people's silence is heard.

A different sort of stage-direction problem, less psychological than technical, is presented by *The Little Tragedies*. How are we to experience those 'time-evacuated' stage cues that call for a process

---

[3] Alexander Dargomyzhsky's *The Stone Guest* (premiered 1872), Nikolai Rimsky-Korsakov's *Mozart and Salieri* (1898), Cesar Cui's *Feast in Time of Plague* (1900), and Sergei Rachmaninov's *Miserly Knight* (1903).

[4] The Falen translation here is of the 1831 version, which, with one scene (3) restored, became the canonical text of the play in the twentieth century. For differences between the two versions of the play, see Chester Dunning with Caryl Emerson, Sergei Fomichev, Lidiia Lotman, and Antony Wood, *The Uncensored Boris Godunov. The Case for Pushkin's Original Comedy with Annotated Text and Translation* (Madison, 2006), 7–14; ch. 4 (pp. 136–56), ch. 6 (pp. 192–236).

but then leap instantly to its results? Examples include Laura's cue '(*she sings*)' in *The Stone Guest*, immediately followed by applause for her completed song, and Mozart's '(*he plays*)' in *Mozart and Salieri*, followed without pause by Salieri's tears shed for the performed Requiem. It would seem that these stylized cues, which register in the head instantaneously but tolerate no true duration, are not the stuff of real staged time and space. Yet *The Little Tragedies*, in their very faithful, very different chamber-opera realizations, have been easily opened up by composers into real performance time at the pivotal moments. Perhaps these playtexts conceal many such accordion-like joints, designed to be realized by competent players the way seventeenth-century musicians realized figured bass in a score. So much seems to us now improbable, glued as we are to the printed canon, but the entertainment halls of St Petersburg were staging gothic spectacles far more imaginative than this. Pushkin spoke eagerly about actors for his as-yet-unapproved *Boris*.

It is possible, of course, that with these dramatic experiments the alchemist-dramatist Pushkin was creating yet another hybrid: a type of play that could be staged, recited out loud, or read to oneself with equal success and all to brilliant effect, but in each case to very *different* effect. This possibility should be allowed to hover over the remainder of the Introduction, which will briefly place each dramatic work in the context of Pushkin's life. Before doing so, we might consider the most extensive surviving commentary by Pushkin on the tasks facing Russian drama in his day: his prefatory remarks to an unpublished review, dated 1830, of another historical drama, Mikhail Pogodin's *Marfa Posadnitsa*.[5] Pogodin was a friend of Pushkin's, a good historian, and his play a rather melodramatic and moralizing exercise on a routine topic: the heroic resistance of Novgorod to Moscow's Grand Prince Ivan III in the late fifteenth century. The play does not merit the generous attention Pushkin gave it, but the comments prefacing the review are of the utmost importance. They suggest how Pushkin hoped the Russians (and specifically his own practice) might fit into European drama, during

[5] 'Notes on Popular Drama and on M. P. Pogodin's *Martha, the Governor's Wife*' (1830), in *Pushkin on Literature*, ed. and trans. Tatiana Wolff (Evanston, Ill., 1998), 263–9.

that fertile year, 1830, that witnessed both the appearance of *Boris Godunov* in print and the writing of the four *Little Tragedies*.

Modern European drama, Pushkin writes, was born in the public square. As a popular form, its primary task had always been to please, entertain, and astonish. Thus drama must never turn tedious; 'the people demand strong sensations, for them even executions are spectacles'. To strive for verisimilitude is a mistake, although in saying this Pushkin did not necessarily endorse the gothic or fantastic; rather, playwrights should feature emotional peaks and high-paced moments. The cruder emotions—laughter, pity, terror, shock—are essential to all dramatic success, high or low. Thus theatre was enfeebled when 'poets moved to court': drama grew decorous, took on problems of state, began to speak pompously and to tremble before high officials. In Pushkin's view, tragedy in Russia had yet to shed its servile tone and rigidity of form. Characters had forgotten how to speak on stage freely, without constraint, and instead of conversations between living people one heard monologues, often broken up into alternating voice-lines but without any true responsiveness or sense of spontaneity. Most dangerous for any playwright was monotony of technique. Even satiric laughter, if applied too predictably, could lose its cleansing force—and murders, if habitual, cease to shock. Didactic moralizing is always inappropriate, Pushkin warns, for it is not the business of the dramatic poet to 'excuse, condemn, or prompt'. Authentic tragedy must be as 'impartial as Fate'. And impartiality can be achieved only if the playwright resolves to 'express the people of the past, their minds, their prejudices' within the value-system of their own time.

Pushkin had long felt that this task was beyond the means of tragedy as presently construed on the European stage. It was also beyond the competence, or the intent, of Romantic playwrights such as Victor Hugo, whose writings *about* drama Pushkin found far more satisfying than the verbose and sentimental plays that Hugo actually authored. One inspiration for dramatic reform that Pushkin explicitly acknowledged was the rising cult of Shakespeare; there is some faint possibility that he knew of Goethe's 1774 *Sturm-und-Drang* drama *Götz von Berlichingen*, with its brief mobile scenes and idiomatic speech. In November 1825, Pushkin finished a play of his own that he titled a *Comedy about Tsar Boris and Grishka Otrepev*, referring to it in letters to his friends as his 'romantic tragedy'. How might this provocative pot-pourri of genre labels—romantic, tragic, comedic—have served Pushkin's turn to history and the Time of Troubles?

Boris Godunov

In the mid-1820s, Russia's encounter with Napoleon and the nation's bristling entry onto the European political stage was still fresh. Russian literature (along with the rest of Europe) was rife with 'Napoleon' tales: the ambitious underling of humble birth who struggles to a position of supreme power, justifying his crimes through appeals to the public good or national glory. Between 1821 and 1824, Nikolai Karamzin, Russia's historian laureate and a close personal friend of the poet, published volumes nine to eleven of his *History of the Russian State*, covering the period from Ivan the Terrible's son Fyodor (r. 1584–98) to the ascension of the False Dimitry (1605). At the centre of these volumes sat the story of Boris Godunov, an untitled boyar, gifted statesman, and elected monarch with a dubious, perhaps criminal past. The failure and then fall of the brief Godunov dynasty (six years of the father, two months of the son) was the formal cause for the country's collapse into its first civil war, the bridge between Russia's two major dynasties.

Throughout 1825, Pushkin was under house arrest at his parental estate of Mikhailovskoe in the Pskov district, south-west of Petersburg. During his previous four years of 'southern exile' Pushkin had been closely watched by the authorities, but he had been relatively free, mobile, in touch with urban culture and in the society of friends. A quarrel with his military superiors and an indiscreet reference to 'atheism' in a private letter subjected the poet to new punitive action. At Mikhailovskoe he was genuinely cut off. The degree of isolation and desolation that marked such provincial exile in pre-telegraph-era Russia, with its impassable roads and dearth of cities, is hard for us to imagine. Nevertheless, it is a thrilling aspect of Pushkin's poetic economy that confinement both infuriated him and stimulated him to unprecedented creative heights. The poet's involuntary 'groundings' were especially productive for his dramatic experiments. Mikhailovskoe was nowhere, but even more distant and desolate was his father's property at Boldino, a village in Nizhny Novgorod province several hundred miles south-east of Moscow. Trapped by a cholera epidemic in Boldino in the autumn of 1830 Pushkin wrote, among much else, his four *Little Tragedies*; confined to Mikhailovskoe a half-decade earlier, he managed to research and write his Boris play in under a year.

Pushkin's primary source was Nikolai Karamzin. But the poet conducted his own research on several sensitive issues. He consulted medieval chronicles as well as accounts by foreign mercenaries, the most important being the Frenchman Jacques Margeret, who entered Russian service in 1600 and served both Tsar Boris and the False Dimitry with distinction. Captain Margeret appears as a character in Pushkin's Scene 16, based on a pivotal (and precisely dated) battle in December 1604, speaking, in French, some famous lines from his own 1607 memoir. Such fastidious historical detail is characteristic of Pushkin as historian and playwright. Like Friedrich Schiller before him, he saw no necessary conflict between dramatic art and accurately documented history. Indeed, certain opinions voiced or enacted in the play—the common people's enthusiasm for the Pretender, Tsar Boris's tyranny and unpopular enserfment policy, the psychology of the crafty Prince Shuisky and the embittered General Basmanov, whose defection to the Pretender sealed the fate of the Godunov dynasty—were better and more boldly researched by Pushkin than by any Russian historian before or since. Here the magnificence of Musorgsky's opera has probably done a disservice to the play. By focusing on the tsar's guilt and the Pretender's Polish love affair (both irresistibly operatic themes), the libretto largely ignores Pushkin's political and military scenes, where so much of the keen intelligence and cutting edge of this historical drama lies.

Of special importance to the poet were his own family papers at Mikhailovskoe. He was intensely proud of the fact that several Pushkins took part in the Troubles, on both sides of the civil war, and two are featured in the play. Gavrila Pushkin (d. 1638), who early joined the Pretender's cause, was re-created quite accurately;

the second 'namesake', Afanasy, was based loosely on two Pushkin brothers who served Godunov. Alexander Pushkin's relationship towards his own surname in the play is a fascinating thread to follow. The exiled poet had no reason to love the reigning Romanov tsar, Alexander I. But he was at the peak of his poetic fame in the mid-1820s and could only covet the status of national poet-playwright, somewhat like the German people's reverence towards Friedrich Schiller, who had died two decades earlier while at work on a Demetrius drama. Such playwrights combine in one person the voice of freedom against oppression, an enlightened helpmeet to rulers, and a prophet of their nation's future greatness. Today's readers of *Boris Godunov* should be alert to the fact that whenever a Pushkin speaks in the play, on either side of the conflict, he voices uncomfortable truths—about serfdom, Boris's reign of terror, support for the Pretender—that were well documented in foreigners' histories and unwelcome as part of the *official* history endorsed by the House of Romanov. 'Oh, how I loathe this rabid [*lit.* rebellious] brood of Pushkins!' the harassed Tsar Boris mutters in Scene 10 as Shuisky enters. As a loyal Muscovite subject and thus spy, Shuisky has just arrived at the Kremlin to report a Pretender in Poland, news vouchsafed to him in confidence the night before by his trusting friend Afanasy Pushkin.

This question of the role of Providence in Dimitry's brief life—and in the long-term life of Russian dynasties—prompts our final comment about *Boris Godunov*, its debts and potentials. Pushkin explicitly named only three influences on his drama: Karamzin, Russian chronicles, and 'our Father Shakespeare'. The Shakespeare connection must be handled with care. From the tragedies Pushkin borrowed little more than the idea of a mixed high and low style, and even that was limited to what survived in the French prose translations available to the poet. There is in Pushkin a compactness, emotional restraint, lack of titanic heroes, and reluctance to bring the supernatural (witches, ghosts) on stage that is altogether alien to *Hamlet*, *Macbeth*, *Othello*, or *King Lear*. It is true that Pushkin, like other Romantic-era playwrights who celebrated Shakespeare, takes pleasure in ignoring the neoclassical unities of time and space. But the feel of his drama is not the feel of a broad, thickly ornamented

Shakespearian canvas, where heroes thunder out monologues on the stormy heath, swords clank and swagger, and atrocities are committed on stage. There is nothing of the gothic in Pushkin's playwriting. His monologues are more often muttered than declaimed. Horrors happen in the wings and are only subtly invoked. Individual scenes respect the trim eighteenth-century convention of only a handful of actors—two, maybe three speaking persons—on stage at one time. When Pushkin labels a protagonist 'Narod', 'the People', we see and hear one face at a time, not a mobbed crowd.

Shakespearian comedy might have contributed something to Pushkin's mixed-style vision in *Boris*, but only indirectly. The one incontestably comic scene, Scene 8, 'An Inn near the Polish Border', with its slapstick monks and incompetent police, took its comedic device of a clever, literate person 'faking a reading' of a criminal suspect's profile in order to save an unjustly threatened life not from the English Bard but from Italian semiseria opera: Act I, Scene 9 of Rossini's 1815 *La gazza ladra* (*The Thieving Magpie*), which Pushkin probably saw staged in Odessa. *Boris Godunov* remains a serious history play. For all of its razor-sharp comic moments, it could never treat national history—its wars, successions, popular sufferings— the way Falstaff does, bumbling, tippling, and womanizing his way through major battles and political watersheds. Shakespearian tragedy and comedy are far less reflected in *Boris* than are the war-saturated chronicle plays, which would have appealed to Pushkin for several reasons. History was dominant over the predictable, privatizing dynamics of guilt or love. A 'Muscovite' chronicle-play could dramatize gratifying analogies between Elizabethan England and post-Napoleonic Russia, two triumphantly rising empires. But what of the ghastly end of *Boris*: one royal house slain, a doomed Pretender on his way to the throne, civil war and invasion in the wings? Contrary to the rising and affirmative spirit of Shakespeare's chronicles, Pushkin brings Russia to the brink of her collapse. Could this really be what the poet meant by Providence?

The answer to that paradox might lie in the fact that Pushkin did not intend his 1825 'Comedy' to be the end. Contemporaries testify that the poet intended at least a trilogy of plays: a *False Dimitry* and a *Vasily Shuisky*, followed by something from the interregnum, that 'would resemble the Shakespearian chronicles'.[6] These sequels would bring the story to its necessary 'providential' culmination, the inauguration of the Romanov dynasty in 1613. In an October 1836 letter to his friend Pyotr Chaadaev, an aristocratic sceptic who denied Russian history any place in the civilized world, Pushkin retorted that Russia had its own 'special mission' and that 'the drama begun at Uglich and concluded at the Ipatiev Monastery' (where the first Romanov tsar, Mikhail, was crowned in 1613) was 'sublime'.[7] Perhaps the sublimity Pushkin had in mind, in the spirit of his early title for the play, was a comedic one: when seen as a single arc, the trajectory of events from 1591 to 1613 was rounded, justified, balanced, triumphant, a shape designed to work out. For comedy, despite its black humour and occasional blood-soaked setback, is always forward-looking, focused on potentials in the present and future that will lead to the birth of the new, as opposed to backward-looking barren tragedy, which it vanquishes. Pushkin experts have argued that the poet's uncompromising insistence on Boris's guilt for the death of Dimitry of Uglich—a hypothesis taken from Karamzin but challenged by other historians, even in the 1820s—can be defended as part of the poet's belief in historical patterning: an unjust dynastic murder, motivated by personal ambition, made possible a new (and glorious) dynasty.[8] Fate was a precious concept to the poet, although he deployed it differently in his dramas than anywhere else.

When Pushkin, illicitly, read his completed 'Comedy' aloud to his friends in 1826, it was a sensation. Upon its publication early in 1831, after a half-decade of delays in the censorship, some scandals, and much fretful tinkering over the text by its author and others, *Boris Godunov* seemed to please no one. It was not recognizable as historical tragedy: the tone was too buoyant, too chatty, and the

---

[6] S. P. Shevyrev, 'Rasskazy o Pushkine', in V. E. Vatsuro et al. (eds.), *A. S. Pushkin v vospominaniiakh sovremennikov*, vol. ii (Moscow, 1974), 40.

[7] Pushkin to Pyotr Chaadaev, 19 Oct. 1836, in J. Thomas Shaw (ed.), *The Letters of Alexander Pushkin* (Madison, 1967), 780.

[8] Such is the argument of Maria Verolainen in 'Dramaturgiia Pushkina', ch. 10 of *The Pushkin Handbook*, ed. David M. Bethea, pp. 190–209, esp. 194–6.

love plot so essential to neoclassical kingship drama was hopelessly
travestied. Nor did the play qualify as 'historical comedy'—that is,
as a treatment of world-historical events from the perspective of a
buffoon or a Falstaff—for its subject matter was too dark, its concerns solemnly dynastic. In Shakespeare's hybrid spirit but with a
neoclassical sense of proportion and purpose, Pushkin had produced
something like a 'tragicomedy of history'.[9] In such a genre, historical
particulars are respected but assumed to fit into a larger frame. The
audience is allowed to glimpse this frame only rarely. Meanwhile, we
must trust to chance and fate. Or as Gavrila Pushkin puts the matter
wisely at the end of Scene 19, watching the defeated Dimitry fall
asleep (and fall out of the play) alongside his dying horse: 'He's in
the care of Providence, it's clear, | And we as well, my friends, must
not despair.'

A Scene from Faust

Boris Godunov remained Pushkin's sole history play. For his later
dramatic projects he turned to legend, biographical rumour, pre-
existing authored works, or stock plots in the European repertory.
All ended up as miniatures: fragments, 'little' tragedies, the
truncated (and perhaps incomplete) masterpiece *Rusalka*. The tiny
Scene from Faust, written in the *Boris* year 1825 but apparently after
the play was finished, is a curious and—for Pushkin's pen—
uncharacteristically cruel fragment. One seeks in vain for substantial, spiritually satisfying links between it and Goethe's complex,
questing hero. But the value of Pushkin's scene does not lie there.
Rather, it exemplifies the poet's skill at filtering a lesser-known
culture and language (German) through successively more familiar
ones (French and English), in order to examine a character-type or
moral scenario of some urgency to his own creative evolution.[10]

---

[9] For more detail, see my ch. 5, 'Tragedy, Comedy, Carnival, and History on Stage',
and ch. 6, 'The Ebb and Flow of Influence: Muffling the Comedic in the Move toward
Print', in Dunning, *The Uncensored Boris Godunov*.

[10] For a comprehensive discussion of this Faust fragment in the context of Russian
Romanticism, see André von Gronicka, *The Russian Image of Goethe*, vol. i, *Goethe
in Russian Literature of the First Half of the Nineteenth Century* (Philadelphia, 1968),
60–74.

Pushkin did not know German and his library contained none of Goethe's work in the original. His upbringing had been rather Germanophobic; his father, Sergei Lvovich Pushkin, was famous for insisting that he would continue to prefer 'Molière to Goethe and Racine to Schiller' despite attempts by some Russian Romantics to push the cause of the German *Sturm-und-Drang* poets. Pushkin the son paid vague but inconclusive tribute to Goethe's genius. His rendering of a seacoast encounter between Mephisto and Faust can best be understood not in connection with Goethe's great drama, but as part of Pushkin's 'outgrowing'—or better, his testing—of a crucial stimulus on his own work and worldview: Lord Byron.

A Scene from Faust brings into dialogue two bestselling types of hero on the literary scene of Pushkin's day: the Devil as gothic villain, and the young man suffering from ennui and Byronic spleen. Both types are corrosive and corruptible. Pushkin's Faust resembles Byron's Manfred (who in turn had been influenced by Goethe's Faust), but the disillusionment and solitary, rebellious pride have now gone further and into even blacker regions. The Devil does what he is always scripted to do in a Faust tale, which is to exploit our deepest anxieties, doubts, cravings for certainty or for pleasure, and then to negate or ridicule their value. The originality of Pushkin's Faust comes into sharp focus in the second half of their dialogue. None of the temporary benefits reaped by Goethe's hero remain operable for him: pursuit of youth, satiety in love, search for knowledge (the natural-science enthusiasms of Goethe never registered on Pushkin at all). What startles us in the scene is the ferocity with which personal boredom and negation degenerate into indifference and then into wanton impersonal destruction. As soon as Faust points out the 'patch of white' on the horizon, Mephisto immediately sinks the ship—for that is why the Devil exists, to carry out our darkest whims. What is destroyed is defined as a ship of fools (with rogues, monkeys, pots of gold, chocolate, syphilis) but its cargo is of no account; in Faust's frame of mind, all humanity is that ship.

Pushkin's Mephisto might profitably be seen, then, as the professional nay-sayer, the world-spirit whose job is to sober us up and to discipline, or perhaps punish, our imagination. It is the Devil's task to expose every human desire and discredit every fond memory ('for boredom thrives on contemplation'). As such he is an image of Pushkin's anti-Muse, that force which makes it impossible to create. And deprived of creativity, Faust—Everyman, Every Poet—finds his energy turning to disgust. To get rid of Mephisto, it is not enough for Faust to declare 'Avaunt thee' and be on his way. Faust is obliged to 'charge him' with an 'assignment', hence the hideous command to sink the first thing that strikes his jaded eye. Byronic spleen, rebellion, and boredom eventually render all matter inert. If *Boris Godunov* is in essence comedic, then *A Scene from Faust* is the darkest possible tragic terrain for a poet, a rare moment of Pushkinian nihilism. None of *The Little Tragedies* can match its metaphysical bleakness.

The Little Tragedies

By 1830, the idea of the dramatized miniature was not new for the poet. In an undated jotting some time during 1826, Pushkin listed ten topics for dramatic consideration: 'The miser', 'Romulus and Remus', 'Mozart and Salieri', 'Don Juan', 'Jesus', 'Berald of Savoy', 'Pavel I', 'the devil in love', 'Dimitry and Marina', and 'Kurbsky'. It is not known for certain why only three of those topics, plus one timely addition, were later realized and loosely grouped in a cycle. We do know, however, that Pushkin attended carefully to omens and thresholds. The autumn of 1830 was one such liminal moment.

In the autumn of 1830, Pushkin (rather to his own surprise) found himself deeply and stubbornly in love. But wedding negotiations were stalled in Moscow. He retreated to his distant estate of Boldino to gather his wits, improve his finances, and write. Quarantined because of an outbreak of cholera, the poet confronted death, the uncertainty (but for him the necessity) of marriage, and perhaps most agonizing, the awareness of his slipping fame with the Russian public, for prose had begun to replace poetry on the literary market. All these pressures conspired to raise his genius to fever pitch. The four *Little Tragedies* can be seen as dramatizations of essential passions (weaknesses, vices, the dark side of certain strengths) that

Pushkin felt obliged to examine, even to exorcize, in order that this threshold be successfully crossed. Bidding farewell to his bachelor life, he worked through his prior encounters with miserliness, envy, lust, and contempt for death, stylizing them by attaching them to a mainstream legend in the European literary tradition.

The last play of the cycle, *Feast in Time of Plague*, stands somewhat apart. It was not on the 1826 list. It does not showcase a personal appetite like envy, greed, or lust—all of which are oriented towards an individualized target and to various degrees graft resentment onto love. Rather it poses a question, surely one prompted by Boldino under the cholera: trapped in a circle of death, which is the more courageous, to revel or to repent? The communal, tableau-like texture of *Feast*, punctuated by speeches, songs, and sermons, contrasts with the more intimate one-to-one tone of the preceding three. Subtitled simply 'from Wilson's tragedy', its source is Act I, Scene 4 of John Wilson's lengthy 'The City of the Plague' (1816), the full text of which was contained in an 1829 anthology of British verse drama published in Paris and part of Pushkin's library.[11] Wilson's melodramatic, rather gothic original opens with two naval officers on the banks of the Thames about to enter plague-stricken London. They encounter a mad prophetic astrologer, several grief-stricken (and beautiful) mourning widows, and a stranger-atheist who confesses that he has blasphemed Christ and mocked death in 'most brutal and obscene song' during grotesque revelries: 'we were lost, yet would we pluck | The flowers that bloomed upon the crater's edge.' This fumy desperation is the starting point for Pushkin's 'edited' version of Scene 4 (shorter than Wilson by 92 lines). Some stretches are rendered quite precisely, others are omitted or creatively mistranslated. To place *Feast* in the context of Pushkin's dramatic plotting, and to sample how the poet extracts from and condenses other playwrights to achieve his own emotional–moral arc, it suffices to look at the Master of Revels.

---

[11] John Wilson, 'The City of the Plague', *The Poetical Works of Milman, Bowles, Wilson, and Barry Cornwall*. Complete in one volume (Paris, 1829), 25–64. Among Barry Cornwall's contributions are fourteen 'Dramatic Scenes', one of which is a three-page sketch entitled 'Juan'. It is very likely that Cornwall's conversational sketches influenced the shape of all the *Little Tragedies*.

Walsingham moves from defiance of death (his 'Hymn to Plagues') to anger and fear (his realization that his debauchery has made him unworthy to join his wife Mathilda in heaven) to confused reflection (the closing stage direction, 'lost in thought'). In Wilson's original, these clashes are far more violent, rebellious, Romantic, 'Byronic'. The Pestilence is routinely compared to slaughter in navy and army battles (with moral preference allotted the Plague, since it is more democratic, killing all ages, male and female). Several revellers accuse the priests of self-serving hypocrisy, and Walsingham, in a God-fearing moment, challenges one young hot-headed atheist to a duel. In contrast, Pushkin's protagonist is a post-Romantic. For all the bravado of his Hymn and the cheering of his fellow revellers, this is no Dance of Death—that honourable, if grotesque, medieval genre designed to reconcile us to our mortality. The evolution of Walsingham from defiant poet sustaining other like-minded rebels, to conscience-stricken widower, to a man who has dismissed the priests and is now 'lost in thought', is a moral trajectory also reflected in the other three *Little Tragedies*. But in those other three, death is not an omnipresent, indifferent condition of the environment; it catches each protagonist unawares. On one level this death is punitive and inevitable, of course—these are tragedies—but the 'crime' being punished in each case is exceedingly complex. There is strength as well as craven hopelessness in it. In each little tragedy, poetry or creativity opposes itself to death in a different way, and the possibility of transcendence is differently linked with humane or redemptive service within a larger community.

Recall what Pushkin had written in his draft review of Pogodin's play earlier that same year, 1830. Laughter, pity, terror, and constant astonishment were essential to all drama. Didacticism was fatal. Tragedy must not preach, it must show; an honest showing forth obliges the playwright to be as 'impartial as Fate'. For a poet like Pushkin, impartiality could be resolved structurally, in the realm of proportion. Bulk or intricacy of explanation is not necessary to it. But balance is always necessary, and each of the first three tragedies is a neoclassically sculpted confrontation that, in the words of one critic, portrays the peak moment or 'fifth act' of a crisis situation that then 'moves swiftly and inexorably to its catastrophic climax'.[12] The crisis breaks, but resolution does not occur. The final stage direction of *Feast in Time of Plague*—'The Master of Revels remains, lost in thought'—is as ambivalent as 'The people are silent' at the end of *Boris Godunov*. Pushkin's closing strategy is to suspend the question rather than answer it. We are left with the two halves of one maximally stressed, but integrated, creative self.

The plot of *The Miserly Knight* was closest to the poet's own biography. Its tensions so closely resembled those between Pushkin and his own frivolous, profligate, tight-fisted parent that the poet presented the piece as his rendering of scenes from an eighteenth-century English 'tragicomedy', *The Covetous Knight* by Chenstone (William Shenstone), even though no such play exists. Albert, the neglected son, is honourable, impulsive, generous, and poor. His father the Baron is a miser of astonishing scope who is determined to protect his coffers of gold from the appetites of his heir. In the final scene, mediated by a congenial and impartial Duke (representing the rights of youth to spend and the duty of wealth to purchase spiritual as well as material goods), the slandered Albert challenges his father to a duel. This sacrilege is interrupted only by the Baron's sudden heart attack and death.

This grim sequence is so melodramatic that it is easy to miss the oxymoron in the title. A true knight cannot be miserly (he can covet, but miserliness is something else). Pushkin understood coveting and to some degree respected it. All strong appetites naturally covet. Pushkin was an extravagant, even a compulsive desirer and spender: of money, energy, women, travel on the road, time in society. So was his father. The difference between Pushkin and his profligate father was that the son, alone in his family, could also create wealth. (Pushkin could stake and gamble away a stack of lyric poems at the card tables because he was capable of more than merely 'winning them back': he could write new ones.) The problem with hoarding—and with the Baron's fantasies—is not the industry involved in accumulating wealth; the Baron, heartless and sadistic as he is, has a

---

[12] Alexander Pushkin, *The Little Tragedies*, trans., with Critical Essays, Nancy K. Anderson (New Haven, 2000), from her 'Introduction', 6.

point when he remarks that getting rich was hard, ascetic work, and let his 'wretched heir' first 'earn the wealth he craves' before he squanders it. The problem with hoarding is its dishonourableness as an economy. Contrary to the claims in his famous monologue, the Baron is not made more secure, serene, powerful, or creative through his chests of gold. Called before the Duke, he reveals himself to be a timid and lying courtier, so much so that according to one critic, *The Miserly Knight* does not qualify as a tragedy at all, but as a satire.[13] After all, greed on stage had been conventionally resolved in a comic fashion. But for Pushkin, comedy alone could not do justice to this theme. He came to admire Shakespeare's moneylender Shylock over Molière's Miser precisely because Shylock displays a complex rather than a simple vice.[14] As a man on the brink of marriage into an impecunious family, and then as the father of four children within six years, Pushkin would feel acutely his duty to provide. He had a rigorous, aristocratic sense of honour. But the equation of money with potency or freedom always remained suspect, a contamination of the muse and a sign that the age of poetry was coming to an end. It would be replaced by an age of iron, of 'dreadful times' and 'dreadful hearts'. Especially odious was money calculated, withheld or locked up. All value, to be valuable, was obliged to circulate.

The same fraudulent idea of creativity as a material good to be calculated and 'paid for' underlies the rival economies of art in *Mozart and Salieri*. In this second little tragedy, however, the antagonists are more perfectly matched and more indispensable to each other. It is a peculiarity of all Pushkin's playwriting that the monologue–confession, designed to acquaint the audience with the anguish and inner sufferings of the hero, does not, as a rule, endear the hero to us; more often than not, words piled on words (even Pushkin's gorgeous words) make us suspicious. There is too much self-centredness in the showcase monologue. Virtue and

[13] Richard Gregg, 'The Eudaemonic Theme in Puškin's "Little Tragedies" ', Andrej Kodjak and Kiril Taranovsky (eds.), *Alexander Puškin: A Symposium on the 175th Anniversary of his Birth* (New York, 1976), 178–95 (pp. 182–3).

[14] In his 'Table-talk' (1836, unpublished) Pushkin wrote: 'Molière's Miser is miserly—and that is all; Shakespeare's Shylock is miserly, resourceful, vindictive, a fond father, witty.' In Wolff, *Pushkin on Literature*, 464.

purposeful activity belong to the responsive, the interruptible, the verbally spare and easily distracted characters: the jesting and accommodating Pretender, the generous but frustrated Albert, the good-natured, straightforward Mozart who enters with a laugh and seems to take more trouble arranging his dinner than writing his Requiem. If Mozart is all lightness and movement, then it is Salieri, heavyweight, who controls the words.

The first scene is given almost entirely in Salieri's zone, framed by two huge soliloquies. Since he is so gifted at self-criticism that is also self-justification, we tend not to doubt his sincerity. But envy—unlike the simpler, one-way passion of miserliness—is two-sided and restless. Its 'hate–love' cannot be trusted. As opposed to the account-keeping Salieri, a 'son of harmony' like Mozart (the musical equivalent of the generously spending, chivalric son Albert) is utterly, unselfconsciously at home in his element. He no more questions his musical gift than a tree in the snowy forest questions the boundless and undeserved energy that will flow into it, come the spring sun. Salieri too is a creator, of course. Although Mozart delights in his rival and includes them together in the 'happy, chosen few', Salieri is gifted enough to know better. He remains an outsider, a 'servant of art' competent to appreciate greatness that he himself cannot create. What is more, this conscientious Viennese pedagogue is obsessed with the fact that Mozart's genius is so very great it cannot be broken down into analysable or teachable parts. Thus it cannot circulate. 'No successor will he leave behind', Salieri laments, because no formula can be extracted from him. Such genius exhausts and depresses us. It belongs to itself alone.

This dilemma would be rich enough, but Pushkin does not rest there. In the second scene, supposedly Mozart's zone, the binary between talent and genius, rule-bound work and undeserved grace, is undone. It is true that Mozart would rather jest or make music than nurse past injuries, but in fact what he talks of in the second scene (the visit of the Man in Black) and the music we hear (a Requiem) are anything but light-hearted or comedic. They are ominous, solemn, and bravely matter-of-fact. The modesty of the true creative artist in the face of death is a major theme in *The Little Tragedies*. That Salieri has been carrying around poison for years on the chance that he would end his *own* life with it might speak in his favour, but Pushkin does not play up this option, nor the hint that Salieri had hoped to drink together with (die together with) his poisoned friend. Salieri recovers quickly from his covert act of murder. For it isn't only 'villainy and genius' that 'sit ill together' but also villainy and genuine, good-spirited laughter. Salieri doubts that Beaumarchais could have poisoned someone, because he was, Salieri insists, 'too droll [*lit.* laugh-filled or comic] a man | for such a crafty deed'. What we notice most about Salieri, both in his monologues and in his morosely self-absorbed exchanges with Mozart, is his absolute humourlessness. In Pushkin's universe, laughter is healthy, humbling, comedic, wisdom-bearing, harmonious; it reduces us to our proper proportions in the world and makes ethical behaviour easier.

With whom did Pushkin identify in this play? Of course great art requires both the winged inspiration of Mozart and the drudging revision of Salieri. But great poets, such as Anna Akhmatova, have argued that Pushkin paired himself with Salieri. The true Mozarts could improvise brilliantly on the spot (Akhmatova had in mind Pushkin's admiration for his friend, the Polish poet Adam Mickiewicz), whereas fastidious workhorses like Pushkin left manuscripts crammed with crossings-out. Again spontaneity, responsiveness, the capacity to seize a cue and transform it into art with no loss of energy or excitement, emerge as central spiritual values for Pushkin the playwright. This argument, that inspired improvisation is the mark of both true poetry and true love, is pursued in the third and longest little tragedy, *The Stone Guest*.

Here too autobiographical resonances abound. Pushkin kept a Don Juan list, womanized indefatigably, and in 1830 must have been intensely curious about the effect of his impending marriage on this heretofore defining aspect of his life. His variant on the Don Juan legend, however, is remarkable for its emphasis on two themes not central to the Molière and Mozart versions and not immediately related to libido: the all-conquering nature of poetry, and the all-consuming rights of the present moment against the claims of memory, loyalty, or a cumulative past. Laura is as much the heroine of the play as Dona Anna. She embodies the absolute present of improvisation, inspiration, and desire. *The Stone Guest* is the most 'performative' of the four tragedies; its four scenes are packed with movement. But these scenes tend to forget one another. In the first, Don Juan has escaped from exile and is planning seduction strategies with Leporello near a monastery. In the second scene, Laura, who— she assures Don Carlos—'never loves two men at once', is a double for Don Juan, whose verses she sings; when Juan actually appears and slays Don Carlos, the two reunited lovers behave as if there had never been a rival. By Scene 3, Laura herself is forgotten. Dona Anna has now become everything—and Don Juan, stripping off one disguise after another, brings her to the brink of a kiss. In Scene 4, the Statue intervenes; the seducer dies uttering Dona Anna's name. In this little tragedy, time works as it does in comedies. The present moment swells to justify every action, without looking back and without regrets.

The death waiting at the end of each of these little tragedies is never a surprise. It is also not very significant. The conflict itself is important, not the outcome, for our psyche contains both antagonists. All those vices—greed, envy, lust, blasphemy in the face of death—have the shadow of virtues clinging to them: envy its awareness of divine injustice; avarice its respect for industry; lust (which is capable of seducing absolutely every living thing) its link with the amoral drives of art; and a reluctance to respect the plague contains within itself the courage not to collapse meekly into death. A true vice is confirmed as such only when it becomes an obstacle to creativity, which is the sole reliable index of immortality. Otherwise, the poet presents the alternatives as impartially as fate. In his final finished drama, *Rusalka*, Pushkin puts aside this complexly double-sided vision of tragedy and creates a new cast of characters in a new sort of space, as superstitious and as non-sentimental as the poet himself, a space where death is not an end. It is scarcely felt as a boundary.

Rusalka

The folkloric story of a maiden seduced, abandoned, with child, who drowns herself in despair and is transformed into a seductive aquatic creature, was popular in Pushkin's era and frequently staged, usually in a comic or sentimental vein. Like *The Little Tragedies*, *Rusalka* was a Russian 'translation' of a pan-European theme. Like all his literary experiments in legend or folklore, Pushkin's sources were predominantly West European, the French translations of the Brothers Grimm (and not, as Soviet-era Pushkin scholars were obliged to repeat, from the poet's much-celebrated Russian peasant nanny). Why Pushkin took up the Water-Nymph story in the early 1830s is unclear. It is true that in 1826 he had fathered an illegitimate son with one of his serfs, Olga Kalashnikova, but about such things young men felt no guilt (embarrassment, but no guilt, especially since the mother was then satisfactorily married off). More likely it was Pushkin's fascination with the challenge of a folk- or fairy-tale drama. It would integrate the supernatural into the realistic but not as Shakespeare did—with witches, ghosts, and a life beyond the grave retaining their power to shock and horrify. Everything would happen more tidily, as in folktales, where there is no oddness registered at all. 'Miracles' and irrational episodes are a routine part of everyday folk life. Death has no power to end anything. The 'dry-ground life' of the seduced and abandoned Miller's Daughter is her prehistory.

The six compact scenes in *Rusalka* cover seven years (as does *Boris Godunov*) and observe the same tripartite shifting geography of home—away—home: first the mill on the Dnieper, where the Miller's daughter is deserted by her Prince; then the Prince's castle, where he and his Princess spend seven childless years; and again home, the Dnieper both underwater and on shore, where the Prince encounters the mad Miller and glimpses Rusalochka, his daughter, sent by her mother to invite him home. So very distant from the comic-operetta mode is Pushkin's treatment of this story that some critics have elevated it to tragedy, albeit of a lyric fairy-tale sort, and claim that Pushkin hoped to stage it as a new dramatic hybrid. Paradoxically, more Shakespearian tragedy resonates in this 'fairy-tale' drama than in *Boris Godunov*. In addition to the drowned Ophelia, there are the chanting *rusalki* who recall the witches in *Macbeth* (in an early draft, not only the voice but the full-bodied ghost of the Miller's Daughter, dripping and green-haired, turns up at the Prince's wedding feast). And framing the whole is *King Lear*: a wilful father who, having lost his beloved (and wilful) daughter, goes mad, and only in his madness can he acknowledge his many years of bad parenting and avarice. Cordelia must die in the Shakespearian scenario, but a water-nymph both can—and cannot. Like an awakened conscience, it is fertile and forever.

We end this introduction with a provocative statement of James Falen's from his own Introduction to his 1990 translation of *Eugene Onegin*. Falen isolates three 'essential clues' to Pushkin's 'artistic nature and to his conception of creativity': his 'sensuality, his courting of chance, and his trust in fate'.[15] Without a doubt, these energies infuse the poet's most marvellous lyrics, several of his longer narrative poems (especially *Ruslan and Lyudmila*), and Pushkin's entire tempestuous life. But it is striking to what extent these values are displaced or deployed differently in the dramas.

Sensuality, for example, is more graphically present as a metaphor for some other desire than for itself. Tsar Boris compares his disillusionment with 'the highest power' to the physical depletion, boredom and coldness after a consummated act of love. The miserly Baron equates visiting his chests of gold with 'a tryst | With some licentious harlot'. Even Don Juan, who is all sensuality, ends up lending his vitality to the spirit of poetry, the ideal of perfect beauty, and the power of the imagination (as Leporello brags of his master) to fill out a 'bit of slender ankle' glimpsed in passing. There is even a certain chasteness in Don Juan, for all that he can seduce every living thing. But more intriguing still in the dramas is the relationship between chance and fate.

It would seem that fate takes all. *The Little Tragedies* are not structured to allow for arbitrariness or chance, since they are largely denouements. *Rusalka* is basically over (she is pregnant and about to be abandoned) before it begins. Only across the broader expanse of *Boris Godunov* might chance have had a freer hand, but even there, once chance events solidify into rumour, the voice of conscience,

---

[15] Alexander Pushkin, *Eugene Onegin*, trans. James E. Falen (Oxford, 1995), p. xii.

or the body of the Pretender, consequences are fated. As we saw, Pushkin had no conceptual problem extending this providential arc to the whole of the Time of Troubles. And here we confront one of the most stunning aspects of Pushkin as playwright.

On the surface his scenes are fatefully closed and one way. But often, at the closing moment, they open up into a question or a paradox. And within each scene, Pushkin has the uncanny dramatic gift of making each actor sound and act free. We the audience do not feel the controlling hand of the author. Rather, we are inside the consciousness of each participant, where motivation appears not self-serving, foolish, or ambitious but simply necessary, the logical way to behave for a person whose access to the world comes solely through that one limited angle of vision. Even the tiniest roles are bathed in this free-standing respect for the individual perspective. In *Boris Godunov*, for example, there is the endearing self-centred chatter of the two old men Mniszech and Wisniowiecki in Scene 12, which makes us smile, and the cocky stand-off between arrogant Pole and Russian prisoner in Scene 18, at which (the stage direction informs us) 'everyone laughs'. Onlookers laugh—in the healthy sense that Pushkin intends—when behaviour makes sense. And behaviour makes sense when it is governed by an honest, delimited self-interest. The miserly Baron, the faithless Prince in *Rusalka*, the cold and ambitious Marina Mniszech, even the poor, denuded, burnt-out Faust are presented so coherently from within their own zones that one involuntarily sympathizes. Pushkin appears incapable of scripting a detached disgust, such as would communicate his abandonment of a character to the realm of caricature. The only possible exception—and it has been found ugly indeed—is his stereotype of the Jewish moneylender Solomon in *The Miserly Knight*. But even there, justification is not denied from within Solomon's own experience and worldview. Solomon is absolutely correct that should Albert die in debt, 'a knight's good word' would be a worthless asset for the 'wretched Jew' who tried to redeem his pledge. With good reason did Pushkin, in his comments on Shakespearian character, single out for special praise Angelo, the duplicitous deputy in *Measure for Measure*, and Shylock, the embittered pawnbroker in *Merchant of Venice*.

In contrast to the lyric, the narrative poem, the prose tale, the history, we might say that the dramatic work exists to illuminate all sides. Antagonists have a right, even an obligation, to act on what they personally see and need. Impartiality, for Pushkin, dictated that there be no single panoptic place from which the spectacle would be wholly true.

TRANSLATOR'S NOTE

EXCEPT for a few drafts and plans for unfinished projects, of which the most substantial is the unfinished prose drama *Scenes from the Times of Chivalry*, the collection given here contains all of Pushkin's dramatic writings. These works by Russia's greatest poet are masterpieces of the European drama, but unfortunately they remain far less known outside Russia than they should be. Only *Boris Godunov* is somewhat familiar abroad through its musical adaptation by Modest Musorgsky in his famous opera of the same name. I hope, therefore, in presenting these translations, to provide readers not only with accurate and poetic versions of these remarkable works, but with texts that might actually be performed in the theatre as well.

Pushkin's first completed drama, *Boris Godunov* (1825), was composed on a large Shakespearian scale, and I have attempted to convey at least some echoes of its linguistic and thematic richness. Although several scenes and parts of scenes are written in prose, the main body of the work is in blank verse of iambic pentameter, which I have followed in this translation. I have not, however, attempted to reproduce those occasional instances where lines are rhymed, since I felt that this would distort both the sense of the words and the flow of the language. As a guide to pronunciation I have placed an accent mark on names and certain other words to indicate where the stress should fall. I should note in particular that the names 'Ivan' and 'Boris' are accented in Russian on their final syllables and are therefore pronounced 'ee-VAHN' and 'ba-REES'.

Pushkin's further experiments in the drama evolved into more compressed and concentrated forms. His next work in the genre was the brief dramatic dialogue, *A Scene from Faust* (1826). It is written in rhymed iambic tetrameter, which I have once again reproduced in my translation. *The Little Tragedies* (1830), those four miniature psychological studies of human passions are composed, like *Boris Godunov*, in blank verse; and many of the plays' passages, supremely effective as drama, are among the glories of the Russian language. With one exception, here too I have followed Pushkin's metrical scheme. In the case of *A Feast in Time of Plague*, however, I have shortened the line from iambic pentameter to tetrameter; this simply seemed to me a better fit as I put Pushkin's words into English.

The last of Pushkin's dramatic works offered here in translation is *Rusalka* (The Water-Nymph), also written in blank verse. Here again, I have preserved the iambic pentameter. The poet worked on the play in the years 1829–32 and several variant drafts exist. It was not published in Pushkin's lifetime and it has generally been regarded as incomplete. Recently, however, an attempt has been made to arrange the scenes in a different order, ostensibly as Pushkin himself would have done, and to argue that the result is a finished work. Whatever the merits of this proposal, I give the play here in its traditional form.

I would like to take this opportunity to thank my colleagues, Natalia Pervukhin of the University of Tennessee, and Caryl Emerson and Michael Wachtel of Princeton University, each of whom read these translations in draft and whose criticisms and suggestions helped to eliminate at least some of their lapses from sense and grace. I am further indebted to Caryl Emerson for the introduction she has contributed to this volume. I also would like to express my gratitude to Judith Luna of Oxford University Press for the extraordinary care and sensitivity with which she has shepherded this book into print.

SELECT BIBLIOGRAPHY

Biography and Letters

Binyon, T., *Pushkin: A Biography* (New York, 2003).
Mirsky, D., *Pushkin* (London, 1926; repr. New York, 1963).
Edmonds, Robin, *Pushkin. The Man and His Age* (New York, 1994).
Shaw, J. T. (ed.), *The Letters of Alexander Pushkin* (Madison, 1967).
Troyat, H., *Pushkin*, trans. N. Amphoux (London, 1974).

General Critical Studies

Barta, P., and Goebel, U. (eds.), *The Contexts of Aleksandr Sergeevich Pushkin* (Lewiston, NY, 1988).
Bayley, J., *Pushkin: A Comparative Commentary* (Cambridge, 1971).
Bethea, D., *Pushkin Today* (Bloomington, Ind., 1993).
—— (ed.), *The Pushkin Handbook* (Madison, 2006).
Bloom, H., *Alexander Pushkin* (New York, 1987).
Briggs, A., *Alexander Pushkin: A Critical Study* (Totowa, NJ, 1983).
Debreczeny, P., *The Other Pushkin: A Study of Pushkin's Prose Fiction* (Stanford, Calif., 1983).
Driver, S., *Pushkin: Literature and Social Ideas* (New York, 1989).
Greenleaf, M., *Pushkin and Romantic Fashion* (Stanford, Calif., 1994).
Kahn, Andrew (ed.), *The Cambridge Companion to Pushkin* (Cambridge, 2006).
Kodjak, A., and Taranovsky, K. (eds.), *Alexander Puškin: A Symposium on the 175th Anniversary of his Birth* (New York, 1976).
—— *Alexander Pushkin Symposium II* (Columbus, Oh., 1980).
Lavrin, J., *Pushkin and Russian Literature* (London, 1947).
Proffer, C. (ed. and trans.), *The Critical Prose of Alexander Pushkin* (Bloomington, Ind., 1969).
Richards, D., and Cockrell, C. (eds.), *Russian Views of Pushkin* (Oxford, 1976).
Sandler, S., *Distant Pleasures: Alexander Pushkin and the Writing of Exile* (Stanford, Calif., 1989).
—— *Commemorating Pushkin: Russia's Myth of a National Poet* (Stanford, Calif., 2003).
Tertz, A. (Sinyavsky), *Strolls with Pushkin*, trans. C. Nepomnyashchy and S. Yastremski (New Haven, 1993).

Todd, W., *Fiction and Society in the Age of Pushkin* (Cambridge, Mass., 1986).

Wolff, T., *Pushkin on Literature* (London, 1971).

On Boris Godunov

Clayton, Douglas, *Dimitry's Shade: A Reading of Alexander Pushkin's Boris Godunov* (Evanston, Ill., 2004).

Dunning, Chester, with Caryl Emerson, Sergei Fomichev, Lidiia Lotman, and Antony Wood, *The Uncensored Boris Godunov. The Case for Pushkin's Original Comedy, with Annotated Text and Translation* (Madison, 2006).

Emerson, C., *Boris Godunov: Transpositions of a Russian Theme* (Bloomington, Ind., 1986).

—— and Oldani, R. (eds.), *Modest Musorgsky and Boris Godunov* (Cambridge, 1994).

O'Neil, Catherine, *With Shakespeare's Eyes: Pushkin's Creative Appropriation of Shakespeare* (Newark, Del., 2003).

Ronen, Irena, 'The Compositional Pattern of *Boris Godunov* and Freytag's Pyramid', *Elementa*, 3 (1997), 195–224.

On The Little Tragedies

Evdokimova, S., *Alexander Pushkin's Little Tragedies* (Madison, 2003).

Pushkin, Alexander, *The Little Tragedies*, trans., with Critical Essays, Nancy K. Anderson (New Haven, 2000).

Further Reading in Oxford World's Classics

Pushkin, Alexander, *Eugene Onegin*, trans. James E. Falen.

—— *The Queen of Spades and Other Stories*, trans. Alan Myers, introduction by Andrew Kahn.

A CHRONOLOGY OF
ALEXANDER PUSHKIN

All dates are given in the Old Style. Russia switched from the Julian to the Gregorian Calendar only after the 1917 Revolution.

1799   Alexander Pushkin is born on 26 May in Moscow to Major Sergei Lvovich Pushkin (1771–1848) and Nadezhda Osipovna Pushkina (1775–1836). On his father's side Pushkin was descended from a somewhat impoverished but ancient aristocratic family. The poet's maternal great-grandfather, Abram Hannibal, was an African princeling who had been taken hostage as a boy by the Turkish sultan. Subsequently brought to Russia and adopted by Peter the Great, he became a favourite of the emperor and under later rulers enjoyed a distinguished career in the Russian military service.

1800–11   He is entrusted in childhood to the care of governesses and French tutors and is largely ignored by his parents. He does, however, avail himself of his father's extensive library and reads widely, especially in French literature of the seventeenth and eighteenth centuries.

1811–17   Attends the prestigious Lycée at Tsarskoe Selo near St Petersburg, an academy newly established by Emperor Alexander I for the education of young noblemen and their preparation for government service.

1814   Makes his debut in print (20 June) with the publication of two poems in the literary journal *The Herald of Europe*.

1815   His lyric poem 'Reminiscences of Tsarskoe Selo' draws the attention of the poets Derzhavin and Zhukovsky, who admire his talent and predict a great future for him.

1816   He meets the historian and writer Nikolai Karamzin as well as Prince Vyazemsky, a poet and critic who will become one of his closest friends and literary allies. He joins Arzamas, the most innovative of the St Petersburg literary societies.

1817   He finishes the Lycée and secures an appointment in the Ministry of Foreign Affairs. The Decembrist conspiracy, calling for the abolition of serfdom and a constitution for Russia, is in its initial stages.

1818   The first eight volumes of Karamzin's *History of the Russian State* are published.

1820   The Emperor Alexander I orders Pushkin's arrest for seditious behaviour (specifically for the poet's politically inflammatory ode 'Liberty'). In July, after the poet's arrest, his mock epic *Ruslan and Lyudmila* is published to considerable acclaim.

1820–4 He is exiled to serve under military supervision in the south of Russia (Ekaterinoslav, Kishinev, Odessa). He travels in the Caucasus, Crimea, and Bessarabia. During this southern period, his 'Byronic' narrative poems *The Caucasian Captive* (1821) and *The Fountain of Bakhchisarai* (1824) are published.

1823   Begins his novel in verse *Eugene Onegin* on 9 May.

1824   Writes narrative poem *The Gypsies*. After further conflict with state authorities he is dismissed from the service and confined to his family's estate at Mikhailovskoe, where he spends two more years in exile.

1825   Chapter I of *Eugene Onegin* published. He completes his first major verse drama, *Boris Godunov*. Death of Alexander I and accession of Nicholas I. Decembrist uprising (14 December), in which several of the poet's friends participated, takes place while Pushkin is still absent from the capital.

1826–31 Freed from exile by the new Tsar Nicholas I (September 1826) and permitted to return to Moscow, he resumes dissipated life. Nicholas makes himself the poet's personal censor.

1826   *Poems of Alexander Pushkin*, Part I published.

1827   The narrative poem *The Robber Brothers* is published. He begins the prose novel, *The Moor of Peter the Great* (never completed), an account of the life and career of his great-grandfather, Abram Hannibal.

1828   Chapters 4 and 5 of *Eugene Onegin* published. Pushkin is placed under surveillance after the dissemination in manuscript of the poem 'André Chénier'. He is further investigated in connection with his blasphemous poem 'The Gabrieliad'. The poet at first denies his authorship of the poem but eventually admits it in a letter to the tsar.

1829   Publication of the narrative poem *Poltava*, celebrating the victory of Peter the Great over Charles XII of Sweden, and of *Poems of Alexander Pushkin*, Part II. He travels to Georgia and the Caucasus and records the experience in *A Journey to Erzurum*. Election to membership in the Society of Lovers of Russian Literature.

1830   Chapter 7 of *Eugene Onegin* published. Pushkin becomes engaged
        to Natalya Nikolaevna Goncharova of a once prosperous family of
        paper manufacturers. While stranded by a cholera epidemic at his
        country estate of Boldino he enjoys an especially productive
        autumn: he completes the final Chapter (8) of *Eugene Onegin*;
        writes *The Tales of Belkin* (prose stories); finishes *The Little
        Tragedies* (*The Miserly Knight, Mozart and Salieri, The Stone
        Guest, A Feast in Time of Plague*); writes *The Little House in
        Kolomna, The Tale of the Priest and his Worker Balda*, and more
        than thirty lyric poems. December: *Boris Godunov* becomes avail-
        able in printed form (in advance of the official publication date,
        January 1831). Crisis point in rebellion of Poles against Russian
        rule; Russian troops on brink of intervention.

1831   January: five years after the completion of his play, Pushkin is
        finally permitted by the authorities to publish a revised version
        of *Boris Godunov*. Marries Natalya Goncharova (18 February).
        Writes *The Tale of Tsar Saltan*. By order of the Emperor Pushkin
        is readmitted to a nominal position in the Foreign Office with an
        annual stipend and is appointed official historiographer.

1832   *Poems of Alexander Pushkin*, Part III published. Birth of his first
        child, Mariya. Begins prose novel *Dubrovsky* (never completed);
        works on his drama, *Rusalka*. Elected to membership in the
        Russian Academy.

1833   *Eugene Onegin* published in book form. Birth of son Alexander.
        Travels to the Orenburg and Kazan districts in connection with
        his research for *A History of the Pugachev Rebellion*. Writes *The
        Tale of the Fisherman and the Fish*, the narrative poem *The Bronze
        Horseman*, the short story *The Queen of Spades*. The finances of the
        Pushkin family, including those of the poet's father, are in a critical
        state; they nearly lose the family property to creditors.

1834   Having been appointed, to his annoyance, as Gentleman of the
        Chamber by the tsar, Pushkin leads a rather unhappy life in court
        circles, is plagued by mounting debts and by his jealousy of his
        wife's admirers. *Andzhelo*, based on Shakespeare's *Measure for
        Measure*, is published. He conducts research for a history of the
        reign of Peter the Great (the work was never completed, although
        his extensive material was published some hundred years after the
        poet's death).

1835   Birth of son Grigory. *Poems of Alexander Pushkin*, Parts III and IV
        published.

1836 Becomes editor of the journal *The Contemporary*, in which his historical novel *The Captain's Daughter* appears. Death of Pushkin's mother (29 March). Birth of his fourth child, Natalya (23 May). Writes a series of religious poems and the final lyric in a cycle of six poems commemorating the friendships he formed at the Lycée.

1837 Incensed by the constant courting of his wife by Baron Georges d'Anthès, a French adventurer in the Russian service, Pushkin challenges him to a duel (an earlier confrontation had been averted when d'Anthès married the sister of Pushkin's wife). The duel takes place on 27 January and the poet is mortally wounded; he dies two days later; and by order of the tsar, who feared disturbances in the capital, his body is taken for burial under cover of darkness to Svyatogorsky Monastery not far from Pushkin's family estate of Mikhailovskoe.

BORIS GODUNOV

To the memory, precious to Russians, of Nikolai Mikhailovich Karamzin, this work, inspired by his genius, with reverence and gratitude is dedicated.

Alexander Pushkin*

HISTORICAL INTRODUCTION

I HAVE not wished to encumber the text of the play with a copious historical annotation, but a brief review of the background and setting will be useful. Somewhat more detailed explanations of specific references are given in the notes at the back of the book.

Pushkin's drama takes place during a period, at the end of the sixteenth and beginning of the seventeenth centuries, that Russians call 'The Time of Troubles', an era of dramatic and violent events. The seeds for these events had been sown in earlier years, in the time of the longest-reigning monarch in Russian history, Ivan IV ('the Dread' or 'the Terrible'). Infamous for his cruelty and debauchery, and the strange piety of his later years, Ivan had fathered three sons with claims to the throne. The eldest, also named Ivan, was his father's favourite and the heir apparent. The tsar, however, in a fit of rage one day, had struck and killed his eldest son with a poker; and so the next in line, Fyodor, a retiring and weak-minded figure, succeeded to the throne upon his father's death. During Fyodor's reign (1584–98), while Boris Godunov was the real power in the realm, Ivan's last living son, the boy prince, Dimitry, died under mysterious circumstances in the town of Uglich.

Although modern scholarship tends to exonerate Boris of any role in the prince's death (the boy actually may have died from a wound he inflicted on himself during an epileptic seizure), Pushkin follows his source, the historian Karamzin, in assuming Boris's guilt. And certainly there were plenty of accusatory rumours rife at the time. In any case, with the young tsarevich no longer alive, the death of Fyodor in 1598 brought to an end Russia's ancient dynasty and ushered in a kind of interregnum and a fifteen-year-long period of rebellion, war, and lawlessness.

The action of the play opens on the death of Fyodor in 1598 and goes on to cover the entire period of the Godunov dynasty. With no living heir to the throne, Boris Godunov, a lesser noble of Tatar descent who had been a close adviser to Ivan IV and the virtual ruler under the weak and reclusive Fyodor, was chosen as tsar by a national council of boyars, church officials, and merchants. As the brother-in-law of the deceased Fyodor and thus a member of the royal family, he had a legitimate claim to the throne, but he had to deal with the resentment and intrigues of envious rivals among the higher nobility, who considered him an upstart. An able, well-meaning, and ambitious man, he had the misfortune to reign (1598–1605) during a period of growing unrest. His abolition of the peasants' right to move from one estate to another (which effectively established serfdom) was unpopular with both peasants and land-owners. Crop failures in the years 1601–3 resulted in widespread famine and led to peasant uprisings. Boris's suppression of his opponents and his brutal campaign against the south-western borderlands made his reign increasingly tyrannical and unpopular. All of this, coupled with the suspicions of his complicity in the young prince's death, gave rise to various plots and challenges to his authority, to which he responded with increasingly harsh and repres-sive measures. When an impostor appeared, claiming to be Ivan's youngest son Dimitry, miraculously escaped from the attempt on his life in Uglich, many dissaffected elements rallied to his cause, particularly disgruntled nobles and the Cossacks of the south-west. In 1604, with some Polish support and a ragtag army of Cossack insurgents and Russian exiles, this 'False Dimitry' crossed the border from Poland and moved against the tsar. After some initial success he was repulsed and forced to retreat; but with the struggle still unresolved, Boris, in April 1605, suddenly died, and his 16-year-old son Feodor succeeded him on the throne. Many of the Muscovite nobles and commanders, however, went over to the Pretender, who in June of 1605, with his Russian supporters and his Polish allies, entered Moscow. The young Feodor and his mother were murdered, and Dimitry was proclaimed tsar. Here, with the cataclysmic close of the short-lived Godunov dynasty, is where Pushkin's play ends, although it was hardly the final chapter in the 'Time of Troubles'.

The Aftermath

Within a year of his accession, Dimitry was assassinated and Prince Shuisky was named tsar. War with Poland ensued; and at the same time, two more False Dimitrys appeared to claim the crown. Marina Mniszech, the ambitious Polish woman who had married the first 'False Dimitry', continued her effort to gain a crown by attaching herself to the second 'False Dimitry' and subsequently to a Cossack rebel chieftain. Various boyar families struggled for supremacy, and rebellious Cossacks as well as Sweden and Poland sought to take advantage of the general anarchy. Shuisky was soon deposed by a boyar faction that then elected Władysław, the son of Poland's King Sigismund, to the throne. Sigismund, however, desired the Russian crown for himself and war with Poland continued amid widespread lawlessness. Finally, a popular uprising drove an occupying Polish army from the Kremlin and, at last, in 1613, the 'Time of Troubles' came to an end with the election as tsar of Mikhail Romanov, who established the dynasty that was to survive for some 300 years, until the Bolshevik revolution of 1917.

CHARACTERS IN THE PLAY*

BORÍS GODUNÓV, a Russian boyar; Regent and later Tsar of Russia

IRÉNA, the Tsarina, widow of Tsar Fyódor (after his death, a nun), sister of Borís

MARIA GODUNÓVA, Borís's wife; on his accession, Tsarina

FEÓDOR, Borís's son

KSENIA, Borís's daughter

KSENIA's nurse

Prince VASÍLY SHÚISKY, boyar of the royal dynasty of Rúrik

Prince VOROTÝNSKY, boyar of the royal dynasty of Rúrik

SHCHELKÁLOV, secretary of the state council

BASMÁNOV, general in Borís's army

Prince MOSÁLSKY, a boyar

AFANÁSY PÚSHKIN, a noble

GAVRÍLA PÚSHKIN, his nephew

SEMYÓN GODUNÓV, relative of Borís, head of his secret police

PATRIARCH, Head of the Russian Orthodox Church

ABBOT of the Chudov Monastery

FATHER PÍMEN, a monk

GRIGÓRY OTRÉPEV, a monk; later the Pretender Dimítry

MISAÍL and VARLÁM, itinerant monks

KHRUSHCHÓV, a Russian adherent of the Pretender in Poland

KARÉLA, a Cossack chieftain

NIKÓLKA, a simpleton

ROZHNÓV, a Russian nobleman captured by the Pretender

HOSTESS of an inn on the Polish border

CZERNIKÓWSKI, a Polish priest

Prince KÚRBSKY, Russian boyar exiled in Poland, son of a great adversary of Iván IV

SOBÁNSKI, a Polish nobleman

MNÍSZECH, Polish military governor

MARINA, his daughter

WISNIOWIÉCKI, Polish nobleman, friend of Mníszech
MARGERÉT and ROSEN, foreign officers in the tsar's service
A POET
Other boyars, servants, soldiers, guests, urchins, voices in the crowd

SCENE 1

The Palace of the Kremlin
(20 February 1598)

The Princes SHÚISKY *and* VOROTÝNSKY

VOROTÝNSKY

We've been assigned to keep the city calm,
But now, it seems, there's no one here to watch:
The Patriarch, and with him all the people,
Have hied them to the convent, seeking news.
How think you this uneasy time will end?   5

SHÚISKY

How will it end? It isn't hard to guess:
The crowd will shed a few more tears... and wail,
Borís will summon up a few more frowns,
Just like a drunk before a cup of wine,
And, in the end, he'll graciously consent,   10
With humbly lowered eyes, to take the crown;
And then he'll be our master as before,
And reign again.

VOROTÝNSKY   But now a month has passed
Since, locked inside the convent with his sister,
He seems to have abandoned worldly cares;   15
And neither Patriarch nor Duma boyars*
Have managed to persuade him from his course;
He pays no heed to tearful exhortations,
To pleas and prayers, to all of Moscow's wails;
He even spurns the Grand Assembly's voice.   20
His sister, too, has been implored in vain
To bless his quick accession to the throne;
The widowed nun-Tsarina* is as staunch
As he himself and equally unbending.
Borís, it seems, has steeled her to his purpose;   25
Perhaps indeed the ruler has grown weary

And shuns the heavy burdens of the state,
Reluctant to ascend the vacant throne?
What say you then?

SHÚISKY   I say it was a waste,
If this be so, to shed Dimítry's blood,   30
For then the prince might just as well have lived.

VOROTÝNSKY

How terrible a crime! But is it true,
Borís gave orders for the prince's death?

SHÚISKY

Who else? Who sought to bribe young Chepchugóv?
Who sent the Bityagóvskys and Kachálov   35
Upon a secret mission? I was charged
To look into the matter at the scene
And there I found fresh traces of the crime;
All Úglich* had been witness to the deed,
Its citizens all testified the same.   40
When I returned, I could have—with a word—
Exposed the hidden villain to the world.

VOROTÝNSKY

Why didn't you destroy him then and there?

SHÚISKY

I must confess that he bewildered me
With unexpected shamelessness and calm;   45
He looked me in the eye and showed no guilt,
Then questioned me on every small detail—
And, face to face with him, I gave him back
The nonsense that he whispered me himself.

VOROTÝNSKY

How shameful, prince.

SHÚISKY   But what was I to do?   50
Reveal it all to Fyódor?* But the Tsar
Saw matters through the eyes of Godunóv,

And listened with the ears of Godunóv.
And what if I'd convinced him of the facts?
Borís would just have turned him round again, 55
And off to some dank dungeon I'd have gone,
Where, soon enough—as happened with my uncle—
They would have had me strangled in the dark.
I mean no boast, but should it come to that,
I have no fear of torture or of death; 60
I'm not a coward... but I'm not a fool
To put my neck inside a noose for nothing.

VOROTÝNSKY

How terrible a crime! But one would think
The murderer must suffer from remorse;
The guiltless infant's blood must be the cause 65
That keeps him from ascending to the throne.

SHÚISKY

He'll not be stopped by that; he's not so timid!
And how he honours us and all of Russia!
Just yesterday a slave and wretched Tatar,
Malyúta's* son-in-law, that bloody butcher, 70
And he himself a butcher in his soul.
He'll grasp the crown and cape of Monomákh*...

VOROTÝNSKY

He's not of noble blood, as you and I.

SHÚISKY

Just so.

VOROTÝNSKY

The names of Shúisky, Vorotýnsky,
Are those of princes nobly born and bred. 75

SHÚISKY

We're royal by our birth... of Rúrik's* blood.

VOROTÝNSKY

But tell me, prince: do we not have the right
To claim the throne as Fyódor's heirs?

SHÚISKY   Far more
  Than Godunóv.

VOROTÝNSKY   So all would say!

SHÚISKY   Well then,
  Should Godunóv not cease his crafty ways,   80
  We might incite the people to rebel,
  To quit Borís and throw their lot with us;
  They've princes of their own from which to choose,
  So let them pick a Tsar among our ranks.

VOROTÝNSKY
  We heirs of Rúrik's line are many still,   85
  But vying with Borís will be a struggle:
  No longer do the people see in us
  An ancient line of warrior potentates.
  We long ago were shorn of our domains,
  And long have served as vassals of the Tsars;   90
  While he, through fear and love, and by his glory,
  Has managed to bewitch the people's hearts.

SHÚISKY (*glancing out of the window*)
  He's had the nerve, that's all; while we... but look:
  The crowd has scattered and returns this way.
  So let's be off, to see if it's decided.   95

SCENE 2

Red Square

The people

A VOICE FROM THE CROWD
  He won't be moved! He's driven from his presence
  All boyars, prelates and the Patriarch.
  They fell before him prostrate, but in vain;
  He dreads the awesome splendour of the throne.

SECOND VOICE
  O Lord! Who'll rule us in these fearful times?   5
  Great woe will come!

THIRD VOICE   But look: the Council Scribe
  Has stepped outside. He'll tell us their resolve.

THE CROWD
  Be quiet! Let the Scribe be heard... he's speaking,
  Let's hear him! Hush!

SHCHELKÁLOV (*from the Red Porch*)*
                      The Council has decided,
  One final time, to see if our entreaties   10
  Can sway our mournful ruler's stricken soul.
  The Patriarch, tomorrow in the dawn,
  Will hold a solemn service in the Kremlin.
  Proceeding then with banners of the saints,
  With icons of Vladímir and the Don,   15
  In company with noble lords and boyars,
  With delegates from Moscow's pious folk,
  He'll once again approach the royal widow,
  Imploring her to pity orphaned Russia
  And consecrate the crown upon Borís.   20
  So go you now, with God, to all your homes;

Give prayer, and may it rise to Heaven's ears,
The solemn supplication of our faith.

(*The crowd disperses.*)

SCENE 3

The Maidens' Field* at the Novodévichy Convent

A crowd of people

FIRST MAN
They've gone to the Tsarina in her cell;
Borís is there as well, with noble lords,
And with the Patriarch.

SECOND MAN   What news?

THIRD MAN   None yet,
He still refuses, but they say there's hope.

A PEASANT WOMAN (*with a child*)
Oh stop your crying! Or the bogeyman   5
Will cart you off! Stop crying now and hush!

FIRST MAN
Why don't we find a way inside the walls?

SECOND MAN
Not likely, friend... the grounds out here are packed,
And there inside as well. You think it's easy?
All Moscow's come... just look: the fences, roofs,   10
The belfry of the church on every floor,
The dome of the Cathedral, every cross—
All tightly jammed with people.

THIRD MAN   Quite a sight!

ANOTHER MAN
What noise was that?

ANOTHER MAN   Look sharp! What noise was that?
The crowd is wailing, falling to the ground,   15
And swelling like a wave in its approach...
It's our turn, brother... quick... get on your knees!

THE PEOPLE (*on their knees, moaning and weeping*)
    Have mercy, father! Take the crown and rule!
    Become our Tsar and father!

FIRST MAN (*in a soft voice*)   What's that wailing?

ANOTHER MAN
    Who knows? We'll let the boyars sort it out,   20
    It's not for us.

THE WOMAN WITH THE CHILD
          What's this? It's time to cry,
  And now he's mute! Here comes the bogeyman,
  So cry, you naughty brat!

        (*She throws the baby to the ground.*
            The infant screams.)

          That's it, just howl.

FIRST MAN
    Since everyone is crying, friend, I think
    We'd better cry as well.

SECOND MAN   I'm trying, brother,   25
    The tears won't come.

FIRST MAN   Me, too... Have you an onion
    To rub our eyes?

SECOND MAN   No luck... I'll spread some spit
    To wet my cheeks... but what was that?

FIRST MAN   Who knows?

THE PEOPLE
    The crown is his! He's taken it at last!
    Borís, our rightful Tsar! Long live Borís!   30

SCENE 4

The Kremlin Palace

BORÍS, *the* PATRIARCH, *and* BOYARS

BORÍS

My holy Patriarch and boyars all,
Before you I have bared my very soul:
You've seen how I assumed the highest power
With humble heart, and with a sense of dread.
How heavy is the burden I must bear! 5
I follow on the throne the great Ivráns,
I follow our lamented Angel-Tsar!...
O Righteous One! O my almighty Father!
Look down from Heaven on Your servants' tears,
And grant the one to whom You gave Your love, 10
The one whom You have raised so high on earth,
Your sacred benediction on his reign.
May I in truth and glory rule my people,
May I be just and bountiful, like You...
I look to you, my boyars, for assistance; 15
Serve unto me as you have served Tsar Fyódor,
Those days when I as well did share your labours,
Before the people's will had made me Tsar.

BOYARS

We will not contravene our solemn oath.

BORÍS

Come with me now—to kneel before the tombs 20
Where Russia's great deceasèd rulers rest.*
And then... we'll call our people to a feast;
And all shall be received as welcome guests,
From mighty lords to blind and wretched beggars.

(*He leaves; the* BOYARS *follow.*)

VOROTÝNSKY (*detaining* SHÚISKY)
  Your guess was right.

SHÚISKY   What guess was that?

VOROTÝNSKY   Why here,   25
  The other day... remember?

SHÚISKY   Not at all.

VOROTÝNSKY
  When all the people went to Maidens' Field,
  You said...

SHÚISKY   It's not a day for recollection, prince;
  Occasions sometimes prompt us to forget.
  And, by the way, those slanders that I spoke   30
  Were only feigned—to put you to the test,
  The better to uncloak your secret thoughts.
  Take heed—the people cheer their new-found Tsar.
  My absence may be seen and taken ill;
  I'll join the rest.   35

VOROTÝNSKY   A courtier of cunning!

SCENE 5

Night. A cell in the Chudov Monastery
(1603)

Father PÍMEN; GRIGÓRY *(asleep)*

PÍMEN *(writing before a lamp)*
    One final tale, one story more to tell,
    And then my chronicle will be concluded,
    My task fulfilled, this duty sent to me,
    A sinner, by our Lord. And not in vain
    Has God so many years made me a witness,   5
    And granted me the art of writing words.
    The day will come when some hard-working monk
    Will find this nameless harvest of my labours,
    And he, like I, will light his icon lamp,
    And, shaking from my words the dust of time,   10
    He'll make a copy of these truthful tales—
    That future men of Christian faith may learn
    The bygone fortunes of their native land;
    That they recall their mighty Tsars of old,
    For all their works, their glory, and their goodness—   15
    And for their sins, their dark and evil deeds,
    They'll humbly ask the Lord to grant them mercy.

    As I decline in age I live anew,
    And ancient days pass once again before me.
    Was it so long ago that they unfolded,   20
    So full of great events, as violent as the sea?
    But now that world is silent and serene;
    My mem'ry has preserved but few who lived,
    And little of their words do I recall.
    All else has vanished in the mist of time...   25
    But day draws near, my lamp is burning low—
    One final tale, one story more to tell.

               (He writes.)

GRIGÓRY (*waking up*)
  The same odd dream! Three times I've had it now!
  Accursèd dream! And there the old man sits,
  Still writing by his lamp. He can't have slept   30
  Or even closed his eyes the whole night long.
  How much I love that peaceful look he wears,
  When, lost in soul amid those ancient times,
  He pens his chronicle. I've often wondered
  Just what he writes with such unflagging zeal: 35
  Of dismal days when Tatar hordes held sway?*
  Of Tsar Iván and bloody executions?
  Of stormy Nóvgorod and its Assembly?*
  The glory of our land? But all in vain,
  His lofty brow and solemn gaze are mute   40
  And give no inkling of his hidden thoughts.
  He's always so—majestic and yet meek;
  Just like a scribe gone grey with all his cares,
  He looks serenely at both right and wrong,
  Sees good and evil with indifferent eyes,   45
  Expressing neither pity nor his wrath.

PÍMEN
  You've woken, brother?

GRIGÓRY   Give me, reverend father,
  Your blessing, please.

PÍMEN   God grant to you his grace
  This day and all the days to come, forever.

GRIGÓRY
  You've been awake and writing all night long,   50
  While I, asleep, have had my rest disturbed
  By hellish dreams, where Satan plagued my soul.
  I dreamt that by a steep and winding stair
  I climbed some tower, from the top of which
  All Moscow seemed an antheap to my eyes;   55
  Below me, on the square, the people seethed,
  All pointing up at me with mocking laughter;

And I became ashamed and full of dread,
And, falling in a headlong plunge... I woke...
Three times I've had this self-same troubling dream.   60
How strange it seemed.

PÍMEN   It's youthful blood at play;
Submit yourself to fasting and to prayer,
And soon your nightly dreaming will be filled
With harmless visions. Even now, my son,
When overcome unwillingly by sleep,   65
If I omit to say my prayers in full,
My old man's rest is neither calm nor sinless;
For often I will dream of rowdy feasts,
Of army camps, or skirmishes at war,
Of all the mad amusements of my youth!   70

GRIGÓRY
What joyfulness you knew when you were young!
You fought beneath the towers of Kazán,*
You served in Shúisky's ranks against the Poles,
You saw the lavish court of dread Iván!
You lucky man! But I, since boyhood days,   75
Have roamed from cell to cell, a wretched monk!
Why shouldn't I enjoy the fun of battle,
Or revel at the banquet of a Tsar?
And then, in ripe old age, I'd be like you:
I'd shun the world and all its vain pursuits,   80
To utter once again monastic vows
And in some quiet cloister lock my soul.

PÍMEN
Do not lament, my son, that you renounced
This sinful world so soon, that few temptations
Were sent you by the Lord. So heed my words: 85
The luxuries and glories of this life,
Like women's love, seduce us from afar.
I've lived long years and had my fill of pleasures,
But never knew true bliss until the Lord

Had led me to the cloister and its peace.   90
Consider, son, the mighty of this earth:
Who's greater than the Tsars? The Lord alone.
Who dares resist them? None. Yet what of them?
The golden crown grows heavy on their brows,
And often they've exchanged it for a cowl.   95
Iván the Dread sought peace and consolation
By living like a monk inside his court.
His palace, full of vain and haughty men,
Took on the aspect of a monastery;
His fearsome guards, in skullcaps and in hair-shirts,   100
By their appearance seemed but docile monks,
And he, the awesome Tsar, their humble abbot.
I saw them all—within this very cell
(Monk Cyril lived here then, a righteous man
Who suffered much. And I as well by then   105
Had learned, by the Lord's grace, the nothingness
Of worldly cares). And here I saw the Tsar,
Wearied by fits of rage, and executions—
Right here—the brooding, silent, dread Iván.
We stood before him, frozen to the ground;   110
He looked at us and quietly he spoke:
'My father monks, the longed-for day will come,
And I shall stand here, thirsting for salvation.
You, Nikodím, and you, Sergéi and Cyril,
You all shall then receive my solemn vow;   115
I'll come to you, condemned for all my sins,
And I shall take the cleansing way of God
And fall before you, fathers, at your feet.'

Thus spoke our mighty sovereign, Tsar Iván,
And all his words flowed sweetly from his lips,   120
And he did weep. And we, in tears as well,
Prayed God that He might send His peace and love
To calm the stormy torments of his soul...
And contemplate his son, Tsar Fyódor, too,
Who sat upon the throne and yearned in vain   125

To lead a silent hermit's humble life.
He made his private rooms a cell for prayer,
Where all the grievous burdens of his power
Would not disturb his shy and saintly soul.
God came to love the meekness of this Tsar,   130
And under Fyódor's reign our Russia thrived
In uncontested glory... At his deathbed,
A strange and wondrous miracle occurred:
Beside his couch, seen only by the Tsar,
Appeared a figure of exceeding brightness,   135
And with this apparition Fyódor spoke,
Addressing him as 'Holy Patriarch';
And those all round were seized by sudden fear,
Aware that he had seen a sacred vision;
For at the time, the high and mighty prelate   140
Was absent from the chamber of the Tsar;
Then, when the Tsar had passed away, the palace
Was permeated with a holy fragrance
And his own face was shining like the sun.
We shall not look upon his like again.   145
O terrible, unprecedented woe!
We've angered God for we indeed have sinned:
We've called a bloody monster to the throne,
A regicide.

GRIGÓRY   I've wanted for some time
    To ask you, reverend father, of the death   150
    Of the Tsarévich. You were there, they say,
    In Úglich at the time.

PÍMEN   Ah, yes, I was!
    God made me witness to an evil deed,
    A bloody crime. To distant Úglich then
    They'd sent me on a mission of some sort.   155
    I came at night. Next morning, during mass,
    The bells rang out; they'd sounded the alarm.
    Commotion, shrieks... men rushing to the palace
    Where our Tsarina lived. I run as well

And find the populace already there.   160
I look about: there lies the slaughtered Prince,
His royal mother fainted at his side;
A nursemaid sobbing with a desperate grief.
The people, filled with rage, are dragging off
The Godless wet-nurse who'd betrayed the Prince...   165
Then, suddenly, that Judas Bityagóvsky
Appeared among them, pale and fierce with malice.
'Look! there's the villain!' cried the mob as one,
And instantly they felled him. Then the people
Pursued three others who had fled the scene;   170
They seized the bloody killers where they hid
And dragged them to the child's corpse, still warm.
Then came a miracle—the body stirred.
'Repent! Confess!' the people screamed at them,
And in their terror of the axe, they did,   175
They made confession... and they named Borís.

GRIGÓRY

How old was Prince Dimítry when he died?

PÍMEN

Some seven years. By now he would have been...
(Ten years have passed since then... no, somewhat more,
Twelve years it is)—He'd be your age, Grigóry...   180
And he'd be Tsar. But God willed otherwise.
And with this woeful story I'll conclude
My chronicle. I've little use these days
For matters of this world. And now, my son,
You've learned to read and write, and so to you   185
I pass along my work; and in those hours
When you are free of prayerful obligations,
Write down, avoiding crafty sophistries,
All things that you shall witness in this life:
Both war and peace, the edicts of our Tsars,   190
The holy miracles of saintly men,
All prophecies and blessèd revelations...
But now my time has come, my time to rest,

To put the candle out... I hear the bells
That summon us to matins... Bless, O Lord,   195
Your servants' lives... my crutch, Grigóry, please.

(*He leaves.*)

GRIGÓRY

Borís, Borís! Before you Russia trembles,
And no one dares to mention or remind you
Of that poor child and his wretched fate.
But here in this dark cell, a hermit monk   200
Condemns you for a hideous transgression;
And you shall not escape the court of man,
No more than you'll escape the court of God!

SCENE 6

The Patriarch's Palace

The PATRIARCH, *the* ABBOT *of the Chudov Monastery*

PATRIARCH He escaped, Father Abbot?

ABBOT Yes, Your Holiness, three days ago.

PATRIARCH The damned scoundrel! Who is he by birth?

ABBOT From the Otrépev clan, descendants of Galician
boyars. He took his vows when he was a youth, I don't know   5
where, and lived for a time in Suzdal, at the Efímev Monastery. On leaving there, he roamed from one cloister to
another, until he ended up among my Chudov brethren. Seeing that he was still young and foolish, I assigned him to the
care of Father Pímen, a meek and gentle elder. He was liter-   10
ate: read our annals, composed prayers to the saints—but,
clearly, his gift for letters didn't come from God.

PATRIARCH These blasted literates! What a thing to say! *I'll be*
the Tsar of Moscow! The devil's spawn, that's what he is! No
need, however, to tell the Tsar of this; why trouble our Sover-   15
eign Father? It will be enough if we inform the councillors
Efímev and Smirnóv of his escape. What heresy! *I'll be the*
Tsar of Moscow!... Catch him, catch him—this devil wor-
shipper—and send him off to Solovétsky,* to banishment and
eternal penance. Why, this is heresy, Father Abbot.   20

ABBOT Heresy, Your Holiness, the rankest heresy.

SCENE 7

The Palace of the Tsar

Two ATTENDANTS

FIRST ATTENDANT
Where is His Majesty?

SECOND ATTENDANT   He's shut himself
Inside his chambers with a sorcerer.

FIRST ATTENDANT
They seem his favourite confidants these days,
These sorcerers, magicians and the like.
He's always seeking omens, like a bride.   5
I wonder what he's trying to uncover?

SECOND ATTENDANT
Well, here he comes. Perhaps you'd like to ask?

FIRST ATTENDANT
How grim he looks!

                          (*They leave.*)

BORÍS (*entering*)   I've reached the highest power;
Six years already have I reigned in peace,
Yet know no happiness within my soul.   10
Just so, in youth, we fall in love and thirst
To drink love's joys; but having quenched this hunger
With nothing but a moment's satisfaction,
We soon grow bored and cold, oppressed once more...
It's fruitless that these sorcerers predict   15
Long life and years of uncontested rule—
I find no joy in power, or in life;
I sense the Heavens' wrath and looming woe.
I know no happiness. At first I sought
To give my people glory and contentment,   20
To win their loyal love with lavish gifts—
But now I've put away that idle hope;

The rabble hate the power of the living,
The dead alone can garner their affection.
We're mad to heed the people's howls or cheers,   25
To let their fickle fancies stir our soul!
When God sent famine all across our land,
And, perishing in torments, people wailed,
I gave them access to the granaries,
I showered them with gold and found them work—   30
But they, enraged, called curses down on me!
When conflagration's flames consumed their houses,
I built them new and better habitations;
And they blamed *me* for all the devastation!
Such is the rabble: seek their love in vain.   35
Within my family then did I seek solace;
I sought my daughter's happiness in marriage,*
But like a tempest, death swept off the groom...
And now a scabrous rumour makes the rounds,
And says the culprit of her widowhood   40
Was *me*, yes *me*, her own unhappy father!
Let someone die... and I'm their secret killer:
I hastened Fyódor to his sorry death,
I poisoned my own sister, the Tsarina,
A gentle nun... I'm guilty of all deaths!   45
I realize now: there's nothing we can trust
To give us peace amid our worldly cares;
There's nothing save our conscience in the end;
A healthy conscience triumphs over all,
It overcomes all wickedness and slander.   50
But if it bears one solitary blemish,
One single stain to make it less than chaste,
Then—woe! As if infected by the plague,
The soul will writhe, the heart will fill with poison,
And, hammer-like, reproach assault the ears;   55
The head will spin, foul nausea take hold,
And visions come of bloody boys... aah, no!...
You long to flee, but nowhere can you go!
Oh, pity him whose conscience is unclean.

SCENE 8

An inn near the Polish border*

MISAÍL *and* VARLÁM, *two itinerant monks;* GRIGÓRY OTRÉPEV *(in layman's attire); the* HOSTESS *of the inn*

HOSTESS What can I offer you, reverend fathers?

VARLÁM Whatever God provides, good lady. You wouldn't have some wine?

HOSTESS How could I not have wine! I'll bring it at once, fathers.   5

(*She leaves.*)

MISAÍL Why so glum, friend? We're finally here—the Polish border you've had such a hankering for.

GRIGÓRY I won't rest easy until I'm in Poland.

VARLÁM What's this love of yours for Poland? Just look at Father Misaíl and me, sinner that I am... ever since we   10 skipped the monastery, it's all the same to us: Poland or Russia, a lute or a flute; just give us some wine, and life'll be fine. And here it comes!

MISAÍL Deftly put, Father Varlám.

HOSTESS (*entering*) Here you are, fathers. Drink it in health.   15

MISAÍL Thank you, dear heart, and may God bless you.

(*The monks drink,* VARLÁM *strikes up the song: 'Down in Kazán, in the town of Kazán'.*)

VARLÁM Why don't you join in the song?... Don't be such a prig; at least take a swig.

GRIGÓRY I don't want a drink...

MISAÍL Free will to the free...   20

VARLÁM And bliss to the drunk, Father Misaíl! Let's raise a glass to the hostess lass. But I have to say, Father Misaíl: a drink in my hand, the sober be damned. It's one thing to tope but another to mope... If you want to live like us, brother, you're welcome here... if not, get out and get lost; a fool is no   25 friend for a priest.

GRIGÓRY Swill if you will, but for God's sake, be still. You see, Father Varlám, I, too, can put things deftly at times.

VARLÁM Why should I be still?

MISAÍL Leave him alone, Father Varlám.   30

VARLÁM What's all this abstinence? Some kind of fast? Remember, he's the one who latched onto us. We don't even know who he is, or where he comes from—and besides, he puts on airs. For all we know, he may have tasted the knout.

(*He drinks and sings: 'A young monk tonsured was.'*)

GRIGÓRY (*to the* HOSTESS) Where does this road lead?   35

HOSTESS To Poland, good sir, to the Luyev Hills.

GRIGÓRY And is it far to these hills?

HOSTESS Not far, you could be there by nightfall, if it wasn't for the Tsar's sentries and the road-blocks.

GRIGÓRY What do you mean, road-blocks?   40

HOSTESS Someone's escaped from Moscow, and they've been ordered to detain and question all travellers.

GRIGÓRY (*to himself*) Here's a mess! Almost free, and disaster strikes.

VARLÁM Hey, comrade! Making eyes at the hostess, eh? It's not   45 vodka you're after, but a lass and some laughter... but that's fine, brother, fine. Each to his own, they say. Now Father Misaíl and I, we've only one yen: to tipple like men, and when the cup's dry, to fill it again.

MISAÍL Deftly put, Father Varlám...   50

GRIGÓRY What do they want, these soldiers? And who fled
from Moscow?

HOSTESS Lord only knows, some thief or bandit, likely, but
now even decent folk aren't allowed to pass, and what will
come of it? Nothing. They couldn't catch a devil in daylight.   55
And as if there wasn't any other way to Poland except by the
highroad! Just turn left from here, take the path through the
woods as far as the chapel by the Chekán brook, then straight
across the swamp to Khlópino, and from there to Zakhárevo,
where any lad can take you to the Luyev Hills. All you ever   60
hear about these cursèd border guards is how they harass
travellers and rob poor folk like us.

(A noise is heard.)

O Lord, what now? Here they come, the cursèd guards, to do
their rounds.

GRIGÓRY Hostess! Is there another room in the tavern?   65

HOSTESS Sorry, dear. I'd be happy to go and hide, myself.
These patrols of theirs are just an excuse to get some wine
and bread and heaven knows what else; may they choke to
death, the damned dogs...

(Some soldiers enter.)

OFFICER Good health to you, hostess!   70

HOSTESS Welcome, dear sirs, make yourselves at home.

FIRST OFFICER *(to one of the others)* Ah! A bit of a party, it
seems, and a chance for some pickings. *(to the monks)* And
who might you be?

VARLÁM We're men of God, humble monks, making our way   75
from village to village, collecting Christian alms for the
monastery.

OFFICER *(to GRIGÓRY)* And you?

MISAÍL Our companion...

GRIGÓRY A layman from this district; I've brought these holy   80
men as far as the border, and now I'm off for home.

MISAÍL So you've changed your mind...

GRIGÓRY (*softly*) Be quiet.

OFFICER Hostess, bring some more wine and we'll have a drink
and a bit of a chat with these venerable men.   85

ANOTHER OFFICER (*in a low voice*) The young fellow looks
pretty threadbare, nothing to be had from him; but these
monks, on the other hand...

FIRST OFFICER Keep it down! We'll get to them now. Well,
good fathers, how's the collecting business?   90

VARLÁM Bad, son, bad! Christians these days have turned
stingy; they love their money, they do, and they hide it.
Don't give much to God. Ah, yes, great sin hath fallen on the
peoples of the earth. Men have become tradesmen and pub-
licans; they think only of their worldly riches and not of the 95
salvation of their souls. You walk for miles on end, begging
with all your heart; and, sometimes, in three whole days you
won't get three whole pence. It's a sin! A week goes by, and
then another, and when you look in your bag, there's so little
in it, you're ashamed to show yourself at the monastery.   100
What can you do? From sorrow and grief, you drink away
what little you've got; it's nothing but wretchedness. Oh, it's
bad, it's bad; the last days have come...

HOSTESS (*weeping*) Lord, have mercy and save us!

(*While* VARLÁM *has been speaking, the* FIRST OFFICER *has
been looking at Father Misaíl ominously.*)

FIRST OFFICER Alyókha! Have you got the Tsar's decree with   105
you?

SECOND OFFICER Right here.

FIRST OFFICER Give it here.

MISAÍL Why do you keep staring at me?

FIRST OFFICER I'll tell you why: a certain wicked heretic, one 110
Gríshka Otrépev by name, has escaped from Moscow. Have
you heard of this?

MISAÍL No, I haven't.

OFFICER So you haven't heard? All right. But by the order of
the Tsar this runaway heretic is to be found, seized, and 115
hanged. Are you aware of that?

MISAÍL No, I'm not.

OFFICER (*to* VARLÁM) You know how to read?

VARLÁM In my youth I could read, but I've lost the skill.

OFFICER (*to* MISAÍL) And you?   120

MISAÍL God didn't make me so wise.

OFFICER Well, here's the Tsar's decree.

MISAÍL What am I to do with it?

OFFICER Seems to me, this runaway heretic, thief and swind-
ler... is you.   125

MISAÍL Me! Merciful Heaven! What do you mean?

OFFICER Stay where you are! Bar the doors. We'll soon get to
the bottom of this.

HOSTESS Oh, these nasty brutes! Won't even leave an old friar
in peace!   130

OFFICER Who here can read?

GRIGÓRY (*stepping forward*) I can read.

OFFICER I'll be damned! Where'd you learn to read?

GRIGÓRY Our sacristan taught me.

OFFICER (*giving him the decree*) Here then, read it aloud.   135

GRIGÓRY (*reading*) 'An unworthy monk of the Chudov Monastery, Grigóry by name, of the Otrépev clan, has fallen into heresy, and, inspired by the devil, has dared to perturb the Holy Brotherhood with all manner of temptations and blasphemies. It has been determined by inquiry that he, the   140 accursed Gríshka, has fled towards the Polish border...'

OFFICER (*to* MISAÍL) What do you mean, it's not you?

GRIGÓRY (*continuing to read*) 'And the Tsar has commanded that he be seized...'

OFFICER And hanged.   145

GRIGÓRY It doesn't say 'hanged' here.

OFFICER That's a lie: not every word gets written down. Read: 'seized and hanged'.

GRIGÓRY 'And hanged... And the age of this thief Gríshka is... (*he looks at* VARLÁM) over fifty. He is of medium stature, has   150 a balding head, a grey beard, and big belly...'

(*All look at* VARLÁM.)

FIRST OFFICER Well, lads, looks like we've found our Gríshka! Take him and bind him. Never would have thought, couldn't have guessed.

VARLÁM (*snatching the paper*) Here, back off, you whoresons!   155 What sort of Gríshka am I? And what do you mean: fifty years old, grey beard and big belly! No, brother, you're too young to pull tricks on me. It's a long time since I've done any reading and I can't make out the words too well, but I'll sure make 'em out this time, now it's a matter of hanging.   160 (*He reads haltingly*.) 'And... the age... of this Gríshka is... twenty.' There, brother, where does it say 'fifty'? You see: 'Twenty'.

SECOND OFFICER That's right, I seem to remember 'twenty' too; that's what they told us.   165

FIRST OFFICER (*to* GRIGÓRY) Seems you're a bit of a joker, brother.

(*During the reading,* GRIGÓRY *stands with lowered head, his hand hidden inside his coat.*)

VARLÁM (*continuing*) 'And of short... stature... broad chested, one arm shorter than the other, blue eyes, reddish hair, with a wart on his cheek and another on his forehead.' And isn't   170 that, friend, a description of you?

(GRIGÓRY *suddenly draws a dagger; everyone falls back from him; he leaps through the window.*)

OFFICERS Stop him! Stop him!

(*All run about in confusion.*)

SCENE 9

Moscow. The house of Prince Shúisky

SHÚISKY, *a party of guests. At supper*

SHÚISKY
We'll have more wine!

(*He and the guests rise.*)

            And now, dear friends and guests,
The final cup! Recite the prayer, my boy.

BOY
O Heaven's Tsar, all-present and eternal,
Receive the prayer of these Thy humble servants:
We all beseech Thee for our mighty sovereign,   5
The righteous man appointed by Thy grace
As Autocrat and Tsar of Christendom;
Preserve him in his palace, and in war,
Upon the road, and on his nightly couch;
And grant him triumph over all his foes,   10
And may his fame resound from sea to sea,
And all his house in health and comfort flourish,
And may its precious branches cast their shade
On all the earth—and unto us, his servants,
May he, as in the past, be bountiful,   15
All-suffering, and full of graciousness;
And may the fountain of his endless wisdom
Forever flow and bathe us in its truth.
And, as we raise our glasses to the Tsar,
So, too, we pray to Thee, the Tsar of Heaven.   20

SHÚISKY (*drinking*)
Long live and reign our mighty Sovereign Lord!
And now, dear friends, I bid you all farewell;
I thank you for partaking of my table

And for your grace. Farewell, and peaceful slumber.

(*The guests leave, he sees them to the door.*)

PÚSHKIN* Alone at last! I'd started to think, Prince Vasíly   25
Ivánovich, that we'd never have the chance to talk in private.

SHÚISKY (*to the servants*) What are you gaping at? Always
eavesdropping on your betters... Clear the table and be
gone... What do you have in mind, Afanásy Mikháilovich?

PÚSHKIN Miracles, no less.   30
Gavríla Púshkin—he's my brother's son—
Has sent me news by courier from Cracow.

SHÚISKY
What news?

PÚSHKIN   Strange news indeed my nephew sends.
The son of Tsar Iván... one moment, wait...

(*He checks to make certain that the door is closed.*)

His son and heir, the boy Borís had murdered...   35

SHÚISKY
There's nothing new in that.

PÚSHKIN   Just wait, there's more.
Dimítry is alive!

SHÚISKY   That's news indeed!
The crown prince* lives! Miraculous for sure.
And is there more?

PÚSHKIN   Just listen, hear me out.
Whoever he may be: the rescued prince,   40
A spirit who assumes his shape and form,
Or even some bold rogue and crass impostor,
It's still the case: Dimítry's reappeared.

SHÚISKY
Impossible.

PÚSHKIN   And Púshkin's seen him, too,
  As he came riding to the royal palace   45
  To make his way, through ranks of Polish lords,
  Into the private chamber of the King.

SHÚISKY
  Who is he, then? Where from?

PÚSHKIN   It's still unclear.
  What's known is this: He served as lowly page
  In Wisniowiécki's house, where, taken ill,   50
  He told a priest-confessor who he was;
  The noble lord, apprised of his strange secret,
  Looked after him and nursed him back to health,
  And took him then to Sigismund the King.*

SHÚISKY
  What say they of this bold and cheeky fellow?   55

PÚSHKIN
  By all accounts, he's affable and clever,
  Adroit in manner, and well liked by all.
  He's quite bewitched our Moscow fugitives;
  The Roman priests and he are thick as thieves;
  He's even won the favour of the King.   60

SHÚISKY
  All that you say, my friend, bewilders me,
  Compels my head to spin with dizzy thoughts.
  There's not a doubt: the man's a rank impostor,
  But poses no small danger, I admit.
  This news is grave! And should the people hear   65
  Or learn of this, a mighty storm will come.

PÚSHKIN
  And such a storm that Tsar Borís may fail
  To keep the crown upon his clever head.
  And serves him right! He rules as did Iván
  (Oh, darken not our dreams with thoughts of him!).   70

What good that public hangings are no more;
That on a bloody stake, for all to see,
No longer do we sing our hymns to Christ;
That we're not burnt alive upon the square,
The Tsar to rake our ashes with his staff?   75
Are our poor lives in any way more safe?
We're threatened every day with some disgrace:
Siberia... the dungeon... or the cowl,
And there in some forsaken place, to die
From hunger or a strangler's knotted rope.   80
And all our noblest houses, where are they?
The Princes Shestunóv, the Sítsky clan,
And Russia's hope, the great Románov princes?*
Imprisoned, or in painful banishment.
And in due course, this fate awaits us, too.   85
This wretched life! Our very homes besieged
By faithless serfs, as if by foreign foes;
All men are spies, now schooled to base betrayal,
All thieves, suborned and purchased by the state.
Our lives are in the hands of any peasant,   90
Whom we may choose to punish as we wish.
And now he binds the serfs in place forever,*
And thus he binds the master to the serf!
No longer do we rule our own estates:
Don't dare to drive away some useless idler!   95
You'll feed him if it pleases you or not;
Don't dare entice a worker from your neighbour!
You'll find yourself in court and charged with theft.
Why, even in the reign of dread Iván,
Such evils never were. And ask the people,   100
If life is better now. Let this pretender
Announce that he'll restore their right of transfer,
And then the fun will start!

SHÚISKY   You're right, good Púshkin,
But on such matters, keep a silent tongue,
Until the time is ripe.

PÚSHKIN   Wise counsel, Prince—   105
   To cloak our minds. You're sensible, I know;
   And I, as always, have enjoyed our talk.
   Should I, at any time, have troubled thoughts,
   I'll hasten to inform you of their cast.
   I have to say, your mead and splendid wine   110
   Have loosed my tongue tonight... Farewell now, prince...

SHÚISKY
   Farewell, my friend... till we two meet again.

          (*He sees* PÚSHKIN *out.*)

SCENE 10

Moscow. The Tsar's Palace

The Tsarévich FEÓDOR *(drawing a map); the Tsarévna* KSENIA;
Ksenia's NURSE

KSENIA *(kissing a portrait)* Sweet prince, my handsome
groom, you came here to Russia for your bride... and you
found instead a frigid grave, far from your native land. O
lamentable fate! I'll weep for thee my whole life long.

NURSE Come now, Tsarévna, hush! A maiden's tears are like   5
the falling dew; when the sun comes up, the dewdrops dry.
You'll have another suitor, a fetching one and kind. You'll fall
in love with him, my pretty, and you'll forget your prince.

KSENIA No, nanny... I'll be faithful to him even though he's
dead.   10

(BORÍS *enters.*)

TSAR
    What is it, Ksenia? Tell me, dearest child.
    A maiden still and like a grieving widow!
    You weep, dear soul, and mourn your vanished groom;
    And I, by fate, have been denied, alas,
    To be the agent of your deepest bliss.   15
    Perhaps I've angered heaven in some way,
    That I could not arrange your happiness.
    Poor innocent, why need you suffer so?
    And you, my son, what's that you're working on?

FEÓDOR
    A map of Muscovy and all its lands,   20
    Our state from end to end. Just look: here's Moscow,
    Here Nóvgorod... and Ástrakhan... and here—
    The sea... the dense and endless woods of Perm;
    And here's Siberia...

TSAR   But what's this here,
This long and winding line?

FEÓDOR   The Volga, father.   25

TSAR
How excellent! Sweet fruit of all your studies!
And look, as from the clouds, one here surveys
Our whole dominion at a glance: its borders,
The towns and rivers. Study well, my son,
For learning brings us earlier to wisdom   30
Than do the lessons of our fleeting life—
The time will come, and soon enough perhaps,
When these domains, these provinces and lands,
Will all be yours to minister and rule—
So study well, my son, that you attain   35
With surer grasp the ways of sovereign power.

(SEMYÓN GODUNÓV *enters*.)

Here comes my Godunóv with his report.

(*to* KSENIA)

And now, my darling, to your chambers go;
Goodbye, my sweet, and may the Lord console you.

(KSENIA *and the* NURSE *leave*.)

What news, Semyón Nikítich?

SEMYÓN GODUNÓV   At first light,   40
Prince Shúisky's steward and a man of Púshkin's
Approached me to accuse the pair of treason.

TSAR
More...

SEMYÓN GODUNÓV
                Púshkin's man gave information first,
Reporting that a courier from Cracow*
Had come to see him—and within the hour,   45
They sent him back, without a written message.

TSAR
  Go seize the courier.

SEMYÓN GODUNÓV   We're in pursuit.

TSAR
  And what of Shúisky then?

SEMYÓN GODUNÓV   Last night at supper,
  He entertained his friends: both Miloslávskys,
  Butúrlin, Saltykóv, and several others,   50
  And Púshkin, too, of course. They parted late,
  But Púshkin, it appears, remained behind,
  And had a long discussion with his host.

TSAR
  Go summon Shúisky now.

SEMYÓN GODUNÓV   He's come himself,
  And waits your pleasure, sire.

TSAR   Then send him in.   55

            (GODUNÓV *leaves.*)

  In league with Poland, eh? What does it mean?
  Oh, how I loathe this rabid brood of Púshkins;
  And neither is this Shúisky to be trusted:
  He seems submissive, but he's bold and cunning...

            (SHÚISKY *enters.*)

  I needs must talk with you of matters, prince;   60
  But you, it seems, have business of your own,
  And so I'll hear you first. What brings you here?

SHÚISKY
  I bring you, sovereign, as my duty bids,
  Important news.

TSAR   I'm listening, go on.

SHÚISKY (*softly, pointing at* FEÓDOR)
　　But, majesty...

TSAR　　　　　　Our son and heir may stay,　　　　　　65
　　To hear Prince Shúisky's information. Speak!

SHÚISKY
　　From Poland, Tsar, comes troubling news...

TSAR　　　　　　　　　　　　　　You mean,
　　The word received by Púshkin out of Cracow.

SHÚISKY
　　He knows of everything!... My mighty lord,
　　I thought this secret still unknown to you.　　　　　　70

TSAR
　　No matter, prince: I need all sorts of tales,
　　To weigh them in my mind; for otherwise—
　　We'll never learn the truth.

SHÚISKY　　　　　　　　I only know,
　　That some impostor has appeared in Cracow;
　　The king and Polish lords support his cause.　　　　　　75

TSAR
　　What say they there? Who is this brash pretender?

SHÚISKY
　　I've no idea.

TSAR　　　　　　What danger does he pose?

SHÚISKY
　　Your power, majesty, is great indeed:
　　Your graciousness, your bounty and your zeal
　　Have won the hearts of all your loyal subjects.　　　　　　80
　　But you yourself must know: the mindless rabble
　　Is fickle, mutinous and superstitious,
　　An easy prey to vain and idle hopes,
　　A slave to every momentary impulse;
　　Indifferent and deaf-eared to actual truth,　　　　　　85

It feeds on fables and on fabrications,
And, in its soul, delights in shameless daring.
So if this unknown vagabond decides
To cross the Polish border into Russia,
The foolish mob will flock to him in droves,   90
Attracted by Dimítry's risen name.

TSAR

Dimítry! Can it be? That boy again!
Dimítry! Aah! Tsarévich... leave us, son.

SHÚISKY

His face is flushed: the storm has come!...

FEÓDOR   But sire,
Will you permit me...

TSAR   No, my son, withdraw.   95

(FEÓDOR *leaves.*)

Dimítry!...

SHÚISKY   So... he didn't know the rest.

TSAR

Attend me, prince: take measures even now
To seal our borders from the Polish state;
Have barricades put up, that not a soul
May pass, that not a raven or a hare   100
Dare cross from Poland into Russia. Go!

SHÚISKY

At once.

TSAR   But wait. This news from Cracow, prince—
Far-fetched, don't you agree? Who's ever heard
Of dead men rising from their sepulchres
To question Tsars, legitimate and rightful Tsars,   105
Anointed and elected by the people,
And crowned in Moscow by the Patriarch?
It's too absurd. But why are you not laughing?

SHÚISKY

   I, sire...

TSAR   But hear me out, Vasíly Shúisky:

   When I first learned the youngster had been...   110

   That this young boy had somehow lost his life,

   You were dispatched to make inquiries; Now

   I charge you by the Cross and in God's name,

   And by your conscience, that you tell the truth:

   You recognized, for sure, the murdered boy?   115

   There'd been no substitution? Answer me.

SHÚISKY

   I swear to you...

TSAR   No, Shúisky, do not swear,

   But tell me plain: Was it the prince?

SHÚISKY   It was.

TSAR

   Attend me well. I offer you forgiveness.

   To punish you for any former lies   120

   Would serve no good. But if you lie today,

   If you dissemble now, on my son's head,

   I swear, that you shall suffer such a death,

   So foul a death, that dread Iván himself

   Will shudder in his grave to see such horror.   125

SHÚISKY

   It isn't death I fear, but your disfavour;

   I wouldn't dare dissemble in your eyes;

   Could I have been so blindly self-deceived,

   As not to recognize Dimítry's person?

   Three days I viewed his corpse in the Cathedral,   130

   In company each time with all of Úglich.

   Around him lay another thirteen bodies,

   The victims torn to pieces by the mob;

   And these already had begun to rot,

   Whereas the prince's boyish face was bright,   135

As fresh and calm as if he merely slept;
And though the gaping wound had not congealed,
His features hadn't altered in the least.
No, majesty, there is no doubt: Dimítry
Sleeps in his grave.

TSAR (*calmly*)   Enough now, you may go.   140

(SHÚISKY *leaves*.)

What anguish in my soul! Let me draw breath...
I felt my very blood, all of an instant,
Rush to my face... and sluggishly recede...
So this is why, for all these thirteen years,
I've kept on dreaming of the murdered child!   145
Yes... yes, that's it! I understand it now.
Who is he, though, my frightful adversary?
Who comes at me? An empty name, a shadow?
And will a shadow wrest from me the purple?
A name—deprive my children of their birthright?   150
I've turned a fool! What's made me tremble so?
Blow at this apparition—and it's gone.
The thing's resolved: I'll show no hint of fear,
But nothing must be taken lightly now...
Oh, heavy lies the crown of Monomákh!   155

SCENE 11

Cracow. WISNIOWIÉCKI's *house*

The PRETENDER *and Father* CZERNIKÓWSKI

PRETENDER

No, father, I foresee no difficulties.
I know the spirit of my people well;
Their piety is not at all extreme:
They hold their Tsar as model of their faith;
And furthermore, they're passive and indifferent.   5
I can assure you that within two years,
All Russia and the Eastern Church itself
Will recognize the rule of Peter's vicar.*

PRIEST

I pray that St Ignatius* be your guide,
When those enlightened days will come at last.   10
Till then, Tsarévich, deep within your soul
Conceal these precious seeds of heaven's grace.
The duties of our faith sometimes require
That we dissemble to the world at large.
The people judge us by our words and deeds;   15
Our true intentions, God alone perceives.

PRETENDER

Amen... Who comes?

(*A* SERVANT *enters.*)

Go say that we'll receive them.

(*The doors open. A crowd of Russians and Poles enters.*)

My comrades all! Tomorrow we depart
From Cracow. I propose, Mníszech, to stop
Three days or so at your place in Sambór.   20
Your castle is renowned, I know, my friend,

Not only for its hospitality
And for the lustrous splendour of its halls,
But for its young and charming mistress, too,
The beautiful Marina, who, I hope,   25
Will greet us there. And as for all of you,
My fellow Russians and our Polish friends,
Together you have raised fraternal banners
Against our common foe, against the villain
Whose cunning has usurped our rightful throne.   30
But now, my brother Slavs, our time has come,
And I shall lead your fierce battalions forth
To join the fight for which we all have longed.
But here, I see new faces in your midst.

GAVRÍLA PÚSHKIN
They've come to beg a sword and, by your grace,   35
To serve you in your cause.

PRETENDER   You're welcome, lads;
Come forward, friends. But, Púshkin, who's that fellow,
That handsome man?

PÚSHKIN
Prince Kúrbsky.*

PRETENDER   Famous name!

(*to* KÚRBSKY)

You're kinsman to the hero of Kazán?

KÚRBSKY
His son.

PRETENDER
Is he alive?

KÚRBSKY   My father died.   40

PRETENDER
A brilliant mind! In war and counsel both.
But since those days when he, a dark avenger,

Redressed, with Polish troops, the wrongs he'd borne,
And moved against the ancient town of Pskov,
All word of him is lost.

KÚRBSKY   My noble father   45
Lived out his life on his Volhýnian lands,*
Awarded him by Poland's King Stefán.*
Secluded there in solitude and calm,
For easement he immersed himself in study;
But peaceful labours brought him no relief: 50
He oft recalled the homeland of his youth
And pined for it until the day he died.

PRETENDER
Unhappy prince! How brightly did it shine,
The dawn of his resounding, stormy life;
But I rejoice, my noble knight, that now   55
His blood, in you, is one again with Russia.
But let our fathers' faults be unremembered;
Peace to their graves! Good Kúrbsky, come... your hand!
The son of Kúrbsky ushers to the throne
The son of Tsar Iván, his father's foe!   60
How strange... but all contrives to my advantage;
Both men and fate contribute to my purpose...
And who are you?

A POLE   Sobánski, Polish noble.

PRETENDER
Let glory shine upon this son of freedom!
And give him in advance one-third his pay.   65
And who are these? I recognize the dress
Of my compatriots. These men are ours.

KHRUSHCHÓV (*bowing low*)
Just so, my sovereign lord. We come from Moscow,
Your diligent, but persecuted, bondsmen.
We feared imprisonment and fled to you,   70
Our rightful Tsar—prepared to give our lives

On your behalf; And may our corpses serve
As stepping stones to lead you to the throne.

PRETENDER

Take heart, you innocent and tortured souls—
Just let me get to Moscow and the Kremlin,   75
And then Borís will pay for all his crimes.
And who are you?

KARÉLA   A Cossack from the Don.
Our fearless troops and valiant hetmen* sent me,
For all the Cossacks of the river Don,
To look upon your shining royal eyes   80
And bow our heads in loyal subjugation.

PRETENDER

I know the Cossack heart and had no doubt
I'd see your mighty hetmen join my ranks.
We thank our faithful subjects from the Don.
We know the Cossack people are oppressed,   85
Unjustly hunted by the Tsar-Usurper;
But if, with God's support, we do ascend
Our forebears' throne, we shall at once bestow
Our favour on the free and loyal Don.

A POET

> (*He draws near, bowing deeply, and takes hold
> of* GRÍSHKA's *robe*.)

Great prince, and scion of a royal house!   90

PRETENDER
What is it, friend?

POET (*handing him a manuscript*)
                    I offer you, my lord,
This paltry fruit of my most earnest labours.

PRETENDER
I don't believe my eyes. It's Latin verse!
What blessings come when sword and lyre unite;

The self-same laurel crowns the brow of both.   95
Though I was born in distant northern lands,
I've long enjoyed the Latin Muse's voice;
I love the shapely flowers of Parnassus,
And prophecies of poets I believe.
The raptures flaming in their ardent breasts   100
Are not in vain. When poets praise our deeds,
They sanctify our purpose in advance!
Approach me, friend. In membrance here of me,
Accept this gift.

                    (*He gives him a ring.*)

                    When Fate's design is done,
And I've assumed my great ancestral crown,   105
I'll look to you and hope to hear once more
Your honeyed voice and your inspired hymn.
*Musa gloriam coronat, gloriaque musam.**
And now, my friends, until the dawn, farewell.

ALL

To arms! We march at dawn! Long live Dimítry;   110
Long live the royal prince of Muscovy!

SCENE 12

Governor MNÍSZECH's *castle in Sambór*
A suite of lighted rooms. Music

MNÍSZECH
  He speaks with no one else but my Marina;
  There's nothing on his mind except Marina.
  And now, it seems, a wedding's in the offing;
  But tell me, friend, could you have even dreamed,
  My daughter would be Muscovy's Tsarina?   5

WISNIOWIÉCKI
  A miracle... And, Mníszech, did you think,
  My former page would mount the Russian throne?

MNÍSZECH
  She's something, my Marina, is she not?
  I gave the merest hint, and said: beware,
  Don't let Dimítry get away. And look: 10
  It's all wrapped up. He's caught within her web.

  (*The musicians play a polonaise. The* PRETENDER *and*
            MARINA *step forward as leading pair.*)

MARINA (*softly, to Dimítry*)
  Tomorrow evening, at eleven then,
  Beside the fountain in the linden walk.

            (*They part. Another couple steps forward.*)

A CAVALIER
  I wonder what Dimítry sees in her?

A LADY
  Why, she's a beauty!

CAVALIER   Yes, a marble nymph;   15
  Her lips are lifeless, and she never smiles...

(Another couple comes forward.)

LADY

He isn't handsome, but his looks are pleasing;
And one can see, he comes of royal blood.

(A new couple)

LADY

But when will the campaign begin?

CAVALIER   Whenever
Dimítry wills. We're ready even now,   20
But he and Lady Mníszech keep us captive.

LADY

A pleasant bondage.

CAVALIER   Yes, of course... if you...

(They separate. The hall empties.)

MNÍSZECH

Ah... we old men no longer dance these days;
The music's thunder stirs our hearts no more;
Nor do we press or kiss a charming hand...   25
Ah, yes, I still recall those jesting days!
But now it's changed, old times have gone for good:
The young today are not so bold, I think;
And beauty, too, seems far less lively now—
Confess it, friend: it's all gone stale and weary.   30
We'll leave them to it, brother. You and I
Will fetch a flask of wine, good Magyar wine,
An ancient vintage, overgrown with moss;
And in a quiet corner, just we two
Will drain the fragrant draught, as thick as oil;   35
And in our cups, we'll ponder many things.
Let's have a drink.

WISNIOWIÉCKI

        You're right, old friend, let's go.

SCENE 13

Night, a garden and fountain

PRETENDER (*entering*)
  And here's the fountain, where she said we'd meet.
  I seem to have been born a fearless man;
  I've looked at death a dozen times or more
  And never did I quake at death's approach.
  At times I've faced imprisonment for life,   5
  I've been pursued—my spirits never faltered,
  And through my boldness I've eluded capture.
  What is it now that so constricts my breath?
  And why these constant tremors in my heart?
  Is this the rush of mad, intense desire?   10
  Oh, no—it's fear. All day in agitation
  I've waited for this meeting with Marina.
  I've thought of all the things that I could say,
  How best I might seduce her haughty mind,
  How I'd embrace her with the name 'Tsarina'.   15
  But now it's time—and I remember nothing,
  No word of all the speeches I've rehearsed,
  For love unhinges my imagination...
  What's that... a sudden gleam... a rustle... hush.
  But, no... it was the moon's deceptive light,   20
  The flutter of a vagrant breeze.

MARINA (*entering*)   Tsarévich!

PRETENDER
  She's here!... O God!... My beating heart has stopped.

MARINA
  Dimítry, is it you?

PRETENDER   Sweet, magic voice!

                    (*He approaches her.*)

You're here at last. Or is it all a dream,
That we're alone, amid this silent night?   25
How slowly did the dreary day roll by!
How slowly did the evening sun go down!
How long I've waited in the gloom of night!

MARINA

Time races by too quick and time is precious.
I didn't make this secret assignation   30
To hear sweet speeches from a lover's lips.
No tender words are needed. I believe
You love me, but I'd rather hear more substance.
You know, Dimítry, that I've now resolved
To join my fate with yours, to share with you   35
The stormy, dark, uncertain days ahead,
But I must know above all else one thing;
And I demand, by right, that you unveil
Your secret hopes and highest aspirations,
And even your most fearful apprehensions,   40
That I might boldly, hand in hand with you,
Set out in life—not blindly, like a child,
Not as the servant of my husband's whims,
A speechless concubine—but as your spouse,
A worthy helpmate of the Russian Tsar.   45

PRETENDER

Let me forget, I plead, for just one hour,
The cares and troubles of that life to come!
And you, yourself, Marina, please forget,
That at your feet is Russia's future Tsar.
Take me, Marina, as your chosen lover,   50
As one whose bliss your glance alone inspires.
Oh, listen to the pleading of my love,
And let me tell you all my heart contains.

MARINA

It's not the time, my Prince. You tarry here,
While your adherents' ardour cools and fades;   55

Each passing day, the hazards and vexations
Grow yet more hazardous and more vexatious.
Already doubting rumours are abroad,
And novelty gives way to novelty,
While Godunóv takes measures of his own.   60

PRETENDER

Why speak of Godunóv? Has he the power
To rule your love, my only joy and bliss?
I now regard his throne and royal might
With passionless indifference and contempt.
What matters glory or the Russian crown,   65
Or life itself—if I'm denied your love?
The poorest hut in distant steppes... and you,
Yes, you alone, would constitute my kingdom;
Your love...

MARINA   For shame! Oh, never, Prince, forget
The high and sacred purpose of your cause: 70
Your majesty and rank are far more precious
Than all the joys and pleasures of this life;
Beside your destiny, all else must pale.
I make this solemn offer of my hand
Not to some rash and love-besotted boy,   75
Insanely captivated by my beauty,
But only to the heir of Moscow's throne,
The prince miraculously saved by fate!

PRETENDER

Don't torture me, my beautiful Marina;
Don't tell me that you choose my majesty,   80
And not myself. You cannot know, Marina,
How painfully your words have stabbed my heart.
But could it be?... How monstrous is the thought!
Speak plain: Had not blind destiny assigned me
The pedigree of Russia's royal house,   85
And were I not the son of Tsar Iván,
The wretched boy forgotten by the world,
Oh, even so—would you still love me then?

MARINA

Dimítry you shall be, and no one else;
I could not love another.

PRETENDER   Stop! No more!   90
I have no wish to share with someone dead
The woman that by rights is his alone.
Enough dissembling; let me tell the truth:
Know then, that your Dimítry long ago
Did die... was buried... and will not return.   95
And would you like to know... who I might be?
I'll tell you then: I'm just a black-robed monk...
When I grew weary of monastic bonds,
Beneath my hood I hatched my daring plan,
Prepared a very wonder for the world—   100
And so at last I fled my dismal cell
And joined the Cossacks in their savage huts.
I learned to ride, and how to wield a sword.
I then came here and called myself Dimítry,
And easily deceived the witless Poles.   105
What say you now, my arrogant Marina?
Does my confession bring you satisfaction?
Why don't you speak?

MARINA   Oh, what a fool I've been!

(*Silence*)

PRETENDER (*to himself*)
I've gone too far; I should have curbed my tongue.
The happiness I've built with so much labour   110
I may have now destroyed beyond repair.
What have I done? I'm mad!

(*aloud*)

                I see... I see:
You feel ashamed of this unprincely love.
Pronounce me, if you will, your fateful word;

My future and my fortune lie with you.   115
I wait your verdict.

(He falls to his knees.)

MARINA   Rise, you poor impostor.
You surely can't imagine that your plea
Will soften this unbending heart of mine,
As if I were a weak and trusting girl?
You're wrong, my friend: I've seen great noble lords,   120
And many famous knights, fall down before me,
But coldly I rejected their entreaties,
And not, I can assure you, for some monk.

PRETENDER *(rising)*
Do not despise a youthful, rash impostor;
He may have hidden virtues after all,   125
That make him worthy of the Russian throne,
And worthy of your precious hand as well...

MARINA
More worthy of the noose, you shameless rogue!

PRETENDER
I'm guilty, yes; with overweening pride
I sought to dupe both God and earthly kings;   130
I've lied to all the world; but you, Marina,
Have nothing to reproach me with, no cause
To punish me, for I have told you all.
I wouldn't have attempted to deceive you,
You were the only creature I adored,   135
Before whose eyes I didn't dare dissemble.
My love, my blind and jealous love of you,
This love alone, compelled me to the truth
And made me speak.

MARINA   What sort of boast is this!
Who asked you, madman, for your grim confession?   140
If you, a nameless vagrant, could succeed
In fooling so completely two whole nations,

You should at least have honoured that success
And kept your bold deception to yourself—
A deep, eternal, closely guarded secret.   145
And how could I commit myself to you,
Forget my noble birth and maiden's pride
To join my fate in confidence with yours?
When you, like some poor simple-headed fool
So mindlessly disclose your own disgrace?   150
It's love, it's love! that makes him babble so!
I marvel that in friendship for my father,
You haven't yet revealed yourself to him;
Or told the king from sheer excess of joy,
Or even Wisniowiécki in your zeal   155
As his most eagerly devoted servant.

PRETENDER

I swear to you, that you, and you alone,
Have drawn this frank confession from my heart.
I swear to you that... never... nowhere else—
Not in the drinking frenzy of a feast,   160
Not with a friend in private conversation,
Not under torture or beneath the knife,
Will I this heavy secret ever tell.

MARINA

You swear! And I'm supposed to take your word.
Oh, yes, I do—but may I ask you, sir,   165
Upon what pledge? The name of God, perhaps,
As fits the Jesuits' adopted son?
Upon your honour as a noble knight?
Or maybe on your kingly word alone,
As royal son. Enlighten me, I pray.   170

DIMÍTRY (*proudly*)

The shade of dread Iván adopted me,
And christened me *Dimítry* from the tomb;
Two nations has he brought to strife around me,
And in my name pronounced Borís's doom.

I am his son, Crown Prince... and I am shamed 175
To stoop before a haughty Polish girl.
So now, goodbye. The bloody game of war,
The vast and heavy duties of my fate,
Will stifle, I can hope, the pangs of love.
And when this shameful passion fades away, 180
I'll loathe you with a passion just as great!
So now I go—to ruin or the crown,
Whichever Russia readies for my head.
And whether I should die, a knight in battle,
Or, like a villain, on the bloody block, 185
I'll not have you as partner and companion,
You'll have no share in what my fate portends.
But in the end, perhaps you may regret
The future you so arrogantly spurned.

MARINA

And what if I expose your bold deception 190
To all the world, before you even start?

PRETENDER

You think I tremble at your idle threat?
What man would heed an unknown Polish girl
Before a Tsar? I tell you, lady, this:
That neither king, nor pope, nor noble lord 195
Cares in the least if what I say is true.
If I'm the prince or not, it's all the same;
I serve as pretext for dissent and war;
That's all they need. And you, my little rebel,
Should understand: they'll crush you into silence. 200
Farewell.

MARINA But stay, Tsarévich. Now at last
I hear a man, and not a mewling boy.
This pleases me and brings us in accord.
Your frenzied outburst I can now forget
And look upon Dimítry once again. 205
But hear me, prince: It's time, it's time; awake!
Delay no more, make haste for Moscow now,

Unseat Borís and seize your rightful throne.
Then send a nuptial envoy here, to me.
But now—I swear by God—until the day　　　　210
You mount the dais of the Russian throne,
Till you have extirpated Godunóv,
I'll hear from you no honeyed words of love.

(She leaves.)

PRETENDER

Far easier to battle with Borís,
Or plot at court with cunning Jesuits,　　　　215
Than with a woman. Damn 'em, they're beyond me.
She twists and turns and slithers all about,
Eludes my grasp, and hisses threats... then stings.
A snake! a snake! No wonder I was trembling.
She almost did me in. But all's resolved:　　　　220
Tomorrow in the dawn, we move our troops.

SCENE 14

The Polish border
(16 October 1604)

Prince KÚRBSKY *and the* PRETENDER, *both on horseback.*
The regiments are approaching the frontier

KÚRBSKY (*reaching the border first*)
Look there! The door to Russia lies before us!
Our Holy Russia... fatherland and home!
With scorn, I shake the dust of foreign soil
From off my clothes—and drink, with greed, fresh air,
My native air!... And now, belovèd father,   5
Be comforted, and in your distant grave
Maý your dishonoured bones rejoice at last.
Our great ancestral sabre gleams again,
The famous sword that conquered dark Kazán,
The mighty sword that serves our Russian Tsars!   10
It revels now in this new feast of war—
To bless our rightful sovereign and our hope.

PRETENDER (*riding quietly, with lowered head*)
How glad he is! And how his spotless soul
Exults in glory and with sparkling joy!
Oh, how I envy you, my valiant knight!   15
Great Kúrbsky's son, brought up in banishment,
Ignoring all the wrongs your father suffered,
You now redeem his sins and ease his sleep,
As you prepare to shed your faithful blood
For his oppressor's son, and thus restore   20
The lawful ruler to your land... You're right:
Your soul indeed should blaze with sweetest joy.

KÚRBSKY
Don't you as well exult in joyful spirit?
There lies our Russia... and it's yours, Tsarévich.

The hearts of all your people wait to greet you;   25
Your Moscow waits... your Kremlin... and your crown.

PRETENDER

Ah, Kúrbsky, Russian blood will flow this day.
You've drawn your sword for Russia, pure in heart,
While I bring men to fight and slay their brothers;
I've summoned Poland to invade our land,   30
And shown our foes the way to precious Moscow!...
But may these sins of mine fall not on me,
But down on you, Tsár-murderer Borís.
We march.

KÚRBSKY   We march... and woe to Godunóv!

(They gallop off. The regiments cross the border.)

SCENE 15

The Council of the Tsar

The TSAR; *the* PATRIARCH, *and* BOYARS

TSAR

    Can this be possible? An unfrocked monk,
    A fugitive, leads rebel hosts against us,
    And dares to write us threats! Enough of this,
    It's time to tame this madman... Trubetskói,
    And you, Basmánov: hasten to the field,   5
    My zealous captains need your help at once;
    Chernígov is besieged by rebel troops;
    Relieve the town and people.

BASMÁNOV   Mighty Lord,
    Before three months have passed, all word and rumour
    Of this impostor will have died away;   10
    We'll drag him here to Moscow in a cage,
    Like some outrageous beast, I promise you,
    I swear by God.

              (*He leaves with* TRUBETSKÓI.)

TSAR   The Swedish king sends word
    And through his envoy offers an alliance;
    But we've no need, I say, of foreign help,   15
    We've troops sufficient to ourselves—enough
    To crush these traitors and their Polish dogs.
    I have declined.
              Shchelkálov, send at once
    To all our district marshals my command:
    To mount their steeds and summon, as of old,   20
    All loyal men to fight for Russia's Tsar.
    And likewise, to the monasteries go,
    And press the clergy's servants to the ranks.
    In former times, whenever danger loomed,

The hermit-monks themselves came forth to battle—   25
But we will not disturb them for the moment;
We ask them for their prayers, and nothing more.
Such is the Tsar's command, and boyars' wish.
And now we face important, grave decisions.
You know that this o'erweening brash impostor   30
Has spread his crafty libels through the land;
His messages, distributed abroad,
Have sown deep doubts and stimulate alarm;
Rebellious whispers haunt the public squares
And agitate men's minds... They must be cooled;   35
I would resist the use of executions,
But what are we to do? We must decide!
You first, your Holiness: disclose your thoughts.

PATRIARCH

Almighty God be praised, your majesty,
That he instilled in you such meek forbearance,   40
That he implanted mercy in your soul.
You would not send the sinner to perdition;
You wait with calm, and hope that these delusions
Will pass away—And pass away they will;
And truth eternal, like the sun, will rise   45
And bless us all.
                    And so, your faithful priest,
Although he has no wisdom of the world,
Makes bold herewith to offer you his view:
This devil's spawn, this cursèd unfrocked monk,
Has made the people think that he's Dimítry;   50
He's cloaked himself with our dear prince's name,
Most shamelessly, as with a stolen vestment...
But strip away this garment—and the fraud
Will shrink with shame in all his nakedness.
And God himself has sent us means for this.   55
Attend, my lord: about six years ago,
The very year when God anointed you
And called you to your most exalted state,

There came to me one day at eventide
A simple shepherd, ancient in his years, 60
Who then relayed to me... this wondrous tale:
 'When I was young,' he said, 'I lost my sight,
And ever after, knew not day from night,
Till ripe old age. In vain I sought a cure
In potent balms and secret incantations; 65
In vain, I sought relief in pilgrimage
To cloisters and to famous wonder-workers;
In vain, I sprinkled on my sightless eyes
The healing waters of our sacred springs—
But God denied my easement and recovery. 70
And so at last, I lost all hope of cure,
And grew accustomed to my darkened world;
And even in my dreams I saw no thing,
But dreamt of sounds alone. And then one day,
While fast asleep, I heard a young boy's voice, 75
That said to me: "Rise up, old man, and go
To Úglich-town, and pray before my grave,
There, in the Church of the Transfiguration.
The Lord is good—and I'll forgive your sin..."
"Who are you, though," I asked the boyish voice. 80
"I am Dimítry, royal prince. The Lord
Hath called me to his Host of Angel-souls,
And made of me a mighty wonder-worker!
So go, old man."... And I awoke, and thought:
What does it mean? Perhaps at this late hour, 85
The Lord at last will grant me my salvation.
And so I undertook the distant journey.
I came to Úglich, where I went at once
To the Cathedral and a holy mass;
And with my zealous soul aflame, I wept... 90
So sweetly that my blindness seemed to flow,
Along with all my tears, out of my eyes.
When mass was done, I asked Iván, my grandson,
To lead me to the grave of Prince Dimítry.
And this he did—and I had scarce begun 95

My quiet prayer before that sacred tomb,
When I recovered sight!... and I could see...
God's world... my grandson... and the prince's grave.'

All this, my lord, is what the shepherd told me.

    (*Agitation among the listeners. During this recitation,*
    BORÍS *several times wipes his face with his handkerchief.*)

On hearing this, to Úglich I did send,   100
And I was told, that many penitents
Had likewise found salvation when they prayed
Before the gravestone of our dear dead prince.
Here's my advice: transfer the holy relics
To Moscow, to the Church of the Archangel;   105
Inter them here, that people clearly see
The base deceit of this ungodly villain;
And then, like dust, his fiendish might will crumble.

        (*Silence.*)

PRINCE SHÚISKY
But who, your Holiness, can know the ways
Of God on high? It's not for me to judge,   110
For He may choose to grant a child's remains
An undecaying sleep and wondrous powers;
But we must be dispassionate and prudent,
And weigh this vulgar rumour with great care.
In such confused and stormy times as these,   115
Won't people say, we've made a holy thing
The instrument of base and worldly ends?
The people waver madly in such matters,
And we've too much of noisy gossip now.
It's not the time to agitate men's minds   120
With such a rash and major innovation.
I do agree: this rumour must be crushed,
This foul apostate and his lies, destroyed.
But there are other means, a simpler way;
And therefore, Tsar, if you should deem it fit,   125

I'll go myself and, in the public square,
Confront the mob and exorcize this madness,
Expose this vagrant and his foul deception.

TSAR

    Let it be so! And now, your Eminence,
    I beg you to attend me in the palace;   130
    I've need of further converse with your grace.

            (*He leaves. The* BOYARS *follow.*)

A BOYAR

    Did you take note, how pale the Tsar became,
    And how his face dripped heavy beads of sweat?

SECOND BOYAR

    I must admit, I didn't dare look up,
    I feared to take a breath, or even move.   135

FIRST BOYAR

    But Shúisky saved the day; thank God for that!

SCENE 16*

A plain near Nóvgorod-Séversky
(21 December 1604)

A battle

SOLDIERS (*fleeing in disorder*) We're lost, we're lost! The Tsarévich! The Polish troops! They're here... They've come!

(*The Captains* MARGERÉT *and Walter* ROSEN *enter.*)

MARGERÉT Stop, you cowards, stop! Allons... Defend zee rear!

ONE OF THE FLEEING SOLDIER Defend zee rear yourself, you rotten heathen. 5

MARGERÉT Quoi? Quoi?

ANOTHER SOLDIER Quack, quack, you foreign frog; quack at the Russian Tsarévich; but we're believers, true Orthodox like him.

MARGERÉT Qu'est-ce à dire 'orsodox?' Sacrés gueux, maudites 10 canailles! Mordieu, mein Herr, j'enrage: on dirait que ça n'a pas de bras pour frapper, ça n'a que des jambes pour foutre le camp.

ROSEN Es ist Schande.

MARGERÉT Ventre-saint-gris! Je ne bouge plus d'un pas— 15 puisque le vin est tiré, il faut le boire. Qu'en dites-vous, mein Herr?

ROSEN Sie haben Recht.

MARGERÉT Tudlieu, il y fait chaud! Ce diable de Pretendair comme ils l'appelent, est un bougre qui a du poil au cul. 20 Qu'en pensez-vous, mein Herr?

ROSEN Oh, ja!

MARGERÉT Hé! Voyez donc, voyez donc! L'action s'engage sur
les derrières de l'ennemi. Ce doit être le brave Basmanoff
qui aurait fait une sortie.   25

ROSEN Ich glaube das.

(*Some German soldiers enter.*)

MARGERÉT Aha! Voici nos Allemands. Messieurs!... Mein
Herr, dites leur donc de se raillier et, sacrebleu, chargeons!

ROSEN Sehr gut. Form up! (*The Germans fall into formation.*)
Marsch!   30

THE GERMANS (*marching off*) Hilf Gott!

(*Fighting. The Tsar's Russians flee again.*)

POLISH SOLDIERS Victory, victory! All glory to the Tsar
Dimítry!

DIMÍTRY (*on horseback*) Sound the cease-fire. We've won.
Enough: Spill no more Russian blood. Withdraw.   35

(*Trumpets and drums resound.*)

SCENE 17

The square in front of one of Moscow's cathedrals

A crowd of people

A MAN IN THE CROWD Will the Tsar be leaving the cathedral soon?

A SECOND MAN The mass has ended; and now the public prayers are taking place.

FIRST MAN Well, did they put a curse on *what's his name?* 5

SECOND MAN I was standing on the porch and heard the deacon cry out: Gríshka Otrépev—anathema!

FIRST MAN Well, they can curse him if they like, but the Tsarévich has nothing to do with Otrépev.

SECOND MAN Now they're singing a requiem for the dead 10
Tsarévich.

FIRST MAN A requiem for someone who's still alive! They'll pay for this one day, these godless blasphemers.

A THIRD MAN Listen! There's some commotion... is it the Tsar? 15

FOURTH MAN No, it's the simpleton.

(*A poor fool enters, wearing an iron cap and draped with chains, surrounded by a band of urchins.*)

THE BOYS Nikólka, Nikólka the Iron-Cap! Boo...

AN OLD WOMAN Leave him alone, you little devils; he's touched by God, he's a holy fool. Pray for me, Nikólka; pray for a sinner. 20

SIMPLETON Gimme a copeck, please... gimme a coin... gimme a coin.

OLD WOMAN Here, old man, here's a copeck for you; remember me in your prayers.

SIMPLETON (*sitting down on the ground and singing*)

> The moon is bright,   25
> The kitty cries,
> O simpleton, arise,
> And pray to God!

(*The boys surround him again.*)

ONE OF THE BOYS Hello, Nikólka, why don't you take off your cap?   30

(*He bangs on Nikólka's iron cap.*)

Oh, how it rings!

SIMPLETON But now I've got a copeck...

BOY You're lying; show it to me.

(*He snatches the copeck and runs off.*)

SIMPLETON (*crying*) They took my copeck; they're mean to Nikólka...   35

THE CROWD The Tsar, the Tsar is coming!

(*The Tsar emerges from the cathedral. A* BOYAR, *preceding him, distributes alms to the beggars. Other* BOYARS *follow.*)

SIMPLETON Borís, Borís, the children are mean to Nikólka.

TSAR Give him some alms. What's he wailing about?

SIMPLETON The children are mean to Nikólka. Cut their throats!... the way you did the young Tsarévich.   40

BOYARS Be off, you fool! Seize the simpleton!

TSAR Let him be. Pray for me, poor Nikólka.

(*He leaves.*)

SIMPLETON (*calling after him*) Oh, no! No prayers for the Herod-Tsar... Our Lady won't allow it.

SCENE 18

Sevsk

The PRETENDER, *surrounded by his followers*

PRETENDER
And where's our captive?

A POLE   Here.

PRETENDER   Then bring him in.

(*A Russian* PRISONER *enters*.)

Your name?

PRISONER   Rozhnóv, a nobleman of Moscow.

PRETENDER
How long a fighting man?

PRISONER   About a month.

PRETENDER
Have you no shame, Rozhnóv—to draw your sword
Against your prince?

PRISONER
                         I had no other choice.   5

PRETENDER
And did you fight at Sevsk?

PRISONER   I came too late,
Arrived from Moscow at the battle's end.

PRETENDER
And what of Godunóv?

PRISONER
                    He's much alarmed
By this defeat and by Mstislávsky's wounding.

And now he's sent Prince Shúisky to the field,   10
To take command and lead the troops.

PRETENDER   But why
Has he recalled Basmánov back to Moscow?

PRISONER
He showers him with honours and with gold
For all his services. Basmánov sits
Within his Council now.

PRETENDER   He'd do more good   15
To join the troops, I'd think. What news of Moscow?

PRISONER
All's quiet there, thank God.

PRETENDER   Do they expect me?

PRISONER
God knows. The people are too much afraid,
And few these days dare speak of you aloud.
Some have their tongues cut off; and some—their heads.   20
Each day, they say, brings one more execution.
The prisons all are crammed and, in the squares,
When two or three convene, some spy slips in;
And then at leisure, in his private rooms,
The Tsar himself interrogates these watchdogs.   25
It's terrible, and best to hold one's tongue.

PRETENDER
A splendid life, you minions of Borís!
How fare the troops? Their mood?

PRISONER   They seem content,
Well clothed and fed.

PRETENDER   And are they strong in number?

PRISONER
God knows.

PRETENDER   Some thirty thousand, would you say?   30

PRISONER

I'd say there's more like fifty, all in all.

(*The* PRETENDER *falls into thought; those around him exchange glances.*)

PRETENDER

Within your camp—what say they there of me?

PRISONER

They talk about your mercy, and they say—
(Now don't be angry)—you're a rogue, and yet
A decent fellow all the same.

PRETENDER (*laughing*)   Well said,   35
And soon enough I'll prove it by my action.
And now, my friends, we mustn't wait on Shúisky;
And so I give you my congratulations:
We fight at break of dawn.

(*He leaves.*)

ALL   Long live Dimítry!

A POLE

We fight at dawn! And they have fifty thousand,   40
While we, at most, no more than fifteen thousand.
The man is mad!

ANOTHER POLE   That's nothing, friend: one Pole
Can challenge hundreds of these Moscow trash.

PRISONER

You're big at talk, but when it comes to fighting,
One Russian sword will put you all to flight.   45

POLE

If you were armed and had your sabre by,
You brazen cur, I'd calm you down with this.

(*He points to his own sabre.*)

PRISONER

> A Russian doesn't need a sword, you dolt.
> So how'd you like a taste of this instead!

(*He shows him his fist.*)

(*The* POLE *looks at him haughtily and walks away
without a word; everyone laughs.*)

SCENE 19

A forest

The FALSE DIMÍTRY *(the* PRETENDER*)*; GAVRÍLA PÚSHKIN

(*In the background lies a dying horse.*)

FALSE DIMÍTRY
Poor noble steed! How gallantly he charged
Into the final struggle of this day,
And, wounded, bore me swiftly to the rear.
My poor, poor horse!

GAVRÍLA PÚSHKIN (*to himself*)
              I don't believe my eyes;
We've lost the battle, and he mourns a horse!   5
A sorry sight.

PRETENDER   Perhaps he's only winded
And weakened from his wound, and... given time,
He may survive.

PÚSHKIN   The beast is done; he's dying.

PRETENDER (*going to his horse*)
My poor, poor horse! How can I help you, friend?
I'll take the bridle off and loose the girth;   10
He'll die in freedom.

           (*He unbridles and unsaddles the horse.*)
           (*Several Polish soldiers enter.*)

           Greetings, gentlemen!
I don't see Kúrbsky with you; where's he gone?
Today I saw him in the thick of battle,
Hacking his way through all the slashing swords
That crowded round him like the waving wheat;   15
But higher than the rest uprose his blade;

His dreadful cry drowned out all other cries.
Where is my valiant knight?

A POLE   Slain on the field.

PRETENDER
Peace to his soul and glory to his name.
How few of us escaped alive, and whole.   20
Those traitors! Cossack villains from the Don.
It's you, you cursèd dogs, that did us in;
You couldn't hold the line for just three minutes!
I'll show them all! I'll have each tenth man hanged.
The brigand scum!

PÚSHKIN   No matter who's at fault,   25
The fact remains: we suffered a disaster;
They routed us.

PRETENDER   And yet, the day was ours:
I'd almost crushed their forward ranks, But then—
The Germans met our charge and threw us back.
They're splendid men, by God, I give them that!   30
I love their courage and I'm much inclined
To form a special guard of these stout men.

PÚSHKIN
But where shall we find lodging for the night?

PRETENDER
What's wrong with here? These woods are good enough.
We'll move at dawn, and be at Rylsk by dinner.   35
Go take your rest.

        (*He lies down, a saddle under his head, and falls asleep.*)

PÚSHKIN   And pleasant dreams, Tsarévich!
A total rout; he saves himself by flight,
And, like a simple child, is unconcerned.
He's in the care of Providence, it's clear,
And we as well, my friends, must not despair.   40

SCENE 20

Moscow. The Palace of the Tsar

BORÍS, BASMÁNOV

TSAR

He's vanquished, but what profit lies in this?
We crown ourselves with but an empty triumph.
Once more he gathers his dispersèd force
And from Putívl's walls makes war again.
And, meanwhile, what do our bold heroes do?   5
They sit at Kromy, where a band of Cossacks,
From crumbling ramparts, merely laughs at them.
What glory!... No, they leave us much displeased.
I'm sending you, Basmánov, to the field;
A man of brains, not birth, will take command;   10
Let pride of place take umbrage and be damned.
It's time to put this high-born rabble down,
To end a mindless and pernicious custom.

BASMÁNOV

Ah, majesty, how blest will be the day
When lists of nobles and their pedigrees,   15
The cause of so much pride and rash dissension,
Go up in flames!

TSAR   That day is near, Basmánov;
But let me first subdue this insurrection
And calm the people.

BASMÁNOV   Pay no heed to them;
The people in their hearts are ever restless;   20
Just so a speeding horse will champ the bit,
A growing boy resent his father's rule;
But all the same, a rider reins his mount,
A father his unruly son commands.

TSAR

> But horses, now and then, unseat their riders,   25
> And sons, in time, escape their fathers' rule.
> Through vigilant severity alone,
> We keep our crown. So thought Iván the Third,*
> A wily Tsar, who smothered all dissent;
> And so his savage grandson thought as well.   30
> The people are impervious to kindness;
> You do them good—they offer you no thanks;
> Ravage and kill—you'll be no worse for that.

> (*A* BOYAR *enters.*)

> What now?

BOYAR   The foreign guests are here, my lord.

TSAR

> I'll go receive them. You, Basmánov, wait;   35
> Stay here till I return. I need to speak with you
> Of other things.

> (*The* TSAR *leaves.*)

BASMÁNOV   A lofty sovereign spirit.
> God grant that he subdue this damned Otrépev.
> He still has much to do before he dies,
> Great things that he'll accomplish for our Russia;   40
> Important plans are stirring in his mind,
> That mustn't be allowed to cool and fade.
> What prospects lie before me when, in time,
> He crushes these disdainful boyar clans!
> I have no rivals on the field of battle;   45
> I'll be the first beside the Tsarist throne...
> And maybe more... But what's that wailing sound?

> (*Commotion.* BOYARS *and* COURT ATTENDANTS *rush about
> in disorder, then gather to exchange whispers.*)

AN OFFICIAL
> Send for a healer!

A SECOND OFFICIAL
             Fetch the Patriarch!

A THIRD
    He's calling for his son, the young Tsarévich!

A FOURTH
    Get him a priest!

BASMÁNOV   What's happened to the Tsar?   50

A FIFTH MAN
    He's taken ill.

A SIXTH   He's dying.

BASMÁNOV   Oh, my God!

FIFTH MAN
    He spoke—then, suddenly—fell from the throne,
    And blood came gushing from his mouth and ears.

        (*They carry in the* TSAR *on a chair. All his household and*
                    all the BOYARS *follow.*)

TSAR
    Go, all of you—let only the Tsarévich
    Remain alone with me.

                    (*All withdraw.*)

                        My death is near;   55
    Come, let's embrace once more... farewell, my son,
    The crown will soon be yours... O God, O God!
    I come before you burdened with my sins,
    Without the time to cleanse my soul with penance.
    And yet I feel, that you are dearer, son,   60
    Than absolution of my soul... so be it!
    A subject I was born and, as it seemed,
    Would die as such, obscure and unremarked.
    But I attained the highest power... How?
    You mustn't ask. You bear no guilt in this,   65

And that's enough: you'll reign by right of birth,
And I alone will answer to the Lord.
O dearest son, beware of all delusions,
And be not blind to lamentable facts.
You take the crown in factious, troubled times: 70
He's dangerous, this mad and strange impostor,
Armed with a great and fearsome name...
I, tutored by my many years in power,
Have known the way to check unrest and strife;
I've made them tremble on their knees before me;   75
The voice of treason didn't dare speak out.
But you... a young, untested judge of men,
How will you govern in this parlous time,
Suppress rebellion and entangle treason?
But God is great! He makes the youthful wise,   80
And gives to weakness—strength. But hear me, son:
Above all else, select a good adviser,
Reliable, mature in years, and cool,
A favourite of the people and a man
Esteemed by boyars for his birth or fame—   85
Prince Shúisky, say. And for the war, you'll need
A skilled commander. Send Basmánov there,
And pay no mind to grumbling from the boyars.
Since early youth you've joined me in the Council;
You know the ways of autocratic rule;   90
Change nothing in the way of things. Tradition
Serves power well. Events have forced me lately
To reinstate beheadings and expulsions—
Abolish these for now, and they will bless you,
The way they blessed your Uncle Fyódor's kindness,   95
When he replaced Iván upon the throne.
And then, in time, you can, by slow degrees,
Retighten once again the reins of power.
Relax them now, but never lose your grip...
To foreign guests, be welcoming and gracious,   100
Accept their services with ready trust.
Observe the canons of the Church with care.

Be taciturn: the Tsar must never speak
In vain, or bandy words on paltry matters;
Like holy bells, his voice must only sound   105
To summon men to sorrow or rejoicing.
O dearest son, you're entering those years
When women's beauty agitates the blood.
Retain, I urge, the chasteness of your soul,
Your pride and dignity, and sense of shame.   110
Whoever in his youth succumbs to vice,
Who revels in voluptuous delights,
Becomes, when he's a man, morose and cruel;
His mind too soon grows sinister and dark...
And always be the ruler of your house;   115
Respect your mother, but as man and Tsar,
Hold sway yourself. Be tender with your sister,
For you will be her sole protector now.

FEÓDOR (*on his knees*)

No, father, live—and reign for many years:
Without you, Russia's lost, and we will perish.   120

TSAR

All's finished now—the darkness dims my eyes,
I feel the coldness of the tomb.

(*The* PATRIARCH *and church dignitaries enter, and behind them
the* BOYARS. *The* TSARINA *is escorted in, supported on
either side. The Tsarévna* KSENIA *is weeping.*)

Who's there?
Ah yes, the vestment... and the holy vows...*
The hour strikes... the Tsar becomes a monk—
A dark and chilly grave to be his cell...   125
A moment more, most holy Patriarch,
I'm still the Tsar... Attend me well, you boyars:
There... there's your Tsar. I call him to the throne.
Basmánov... kiss the Cross... protect Feódor...
And you, my friends, I beg you from my deathbed   130
To serve my son with zealousness and truth!

He's still so young, and innocent of soul.
Will you so swear?

BOYARS   We swear.

TSAR   Then I'm content.
Forgive me my temptations and my sins,
My deep offences and my hidden crimes...   135
Approach me, holy father, I'm prepared.

(*The rite of tonsuring begins: the* TSAR *takes monastic vows.*
The women, in a faint, are carried out.)

SCENE 21

Russian Army Headquarters

(BASMÁNOV *shows* PÚSHKIN *into his tent.*)

BASMÁNOV
Come in, and feel completely free to speak.
So then, he's sent you here to parley, has he?

GAVRÍLA PÚSHKIN
He offers you his friendship and regard...
Supreme position in the Russian realm.

BASMÁNOV
But I already have supreme position: 5
The youthful Tsar has made me his commander;
On my behalf, he spurned both ranking nobles
And boyar wrath. I've given him my oath.

PÚSHKIN
You gave your oath to Russia's legal heir;
But if another claimant were alive,   10
More legal yet?

BASMÁNOV   Come Púshkin, that's enough:
I know precisely who he is, so please,
Stop playing games!

PÚSHKIN   Both Poland and our Russia
Have long accepted him as Prince Dimítry;
But I, in any case, don't press the point.   15
Perhaps he is Dimítry after all,
Or maybe a pretender, as you claim;
I only know that one of these fine days,
Borís's son will yield him Moscow's throne.

BASMÁNOV
So long as I support the youthful Tsar,   20

So long will he remain upon his throne;
We have sufficient troops, thank God for that,
And with a victory I can give them heart.
And whom do you propose to send against me?
That Cossack átaman Karéla? Mníszech?   25
At most you've got eight thousand troops, no more.

PÚSHKIN
You're wrong: we haven't near that many men.
I'll tell you frankly that our troops are trash.
The Cossacks only raid and pillage towns,
The Poles just brag and fill themselves with drink;   30
Our Russians?... not much there to cheer about...
I won't be clever here and try to trick you.
You want to know, Basmánov, where we're strong?
Not in our troops, not in our Polish allies,
But in men's minds, in what the people prize!   35
And surely you recall our easy conquests,
The peaceful triumphs that Dimítry's won;
How, everywhere, without a single shot,
Whole towns and cities have surrendered meekly,
Their leaders who resisted—bound and gagged.   40
And was it willingly your troops went forth
To fight against him? Where was that, I ask.
And this was under Godunóv! And now?!
So give it up, Basmánov; it's too late
To fan the ashes of this dying war.   45
With all your brains and all your firm resolve,
You won't prevail. And wouldn't it be better
For you to make a sensible decision,
To be the first to name Dimítry Tsar?
If you do this, you'll make him friend for life.   50
What do you think?

BASMÁNOV   I'll let you know tomorrow.

PÚSHKIN
Be wise.

BASMÁNOV
          Goodbye.

PÚSHKIN   Think hard on this, Basmánov.

                    (PÚSHKIN *leaves*.)

BASMÁNOV
    He's right, I know. All round us treason ripens.
    But what to do? If I delay too long,
    These rebels may deliver me in chains   55
    To this Otrépev. Should I make a truce,
    Forestall the stormy surging of this flood,
    And go myself?... But this betrays my oath!
    And earns me shame through all the generations;
    Repays my youthful master for his trust   60
    With such a base and terrible betrayal...
    It's easy for this banished renegade
    To plot sedition and foment revolt,
    But how can I, the favourite of the Tsar...
    But death... and power... and the people's needs...   65

                    (*He ponders*.)

Where are my men?

                    (*He gives a whistle*.)

                    My horse! Sound the alert!

SCENE 22

Moscow. The Place of Proclamations*

(PÚSHKIN *enters, surrounded by a crowd.*)

A VOICE FROM THE CROWD
Dimítry's sent a boyar with a message.
Let's hear what the Tsarévich has to say.
This way! Up here!

PÚSHKIN (*from the platform*)
      You citizens of Moscow,
I bring you greetings from your own Tsarévich.

     (*He bows to them.*)

You know that through the providence of God   5
Our Prince survived the foul assassin's blade.
He came to bring an evil man to justice,
But now Borís lies stricken by the Lord;
All Russia has submitted to Dimítry.
Basmánov, too, with deep and vast repentance,   10
Has brought the troops to swear him their allegiance.
Dimítry comes to you in love and peace;
Would you, to please the house of Godunóv,
Upraise you hand against your lawful Tsar,
The progeny and heir of Monomákh?   15

THE PEOPLE
We wouldn't, no.

PÚSHKIN   You citizens of Moscow!
The world knows well the burdens you have borne
Beneath the yoke of that malign usurper:
Dishonour, death, imprisonment, taxation,
Harsh labour, hunger—all of these you've suffered.   20
Dimítry is disposed to show his favour—
To boyars, nobles, men-at-arms, officials;

To merchants, foreign guests—to all good people.
Are you so madly obdurate and proud
That you would flee these kindnesses he offers?   25
But now he comes—and with a mighty force—
To claim his seat on his ancestral throne.
Be feared of God, and anger not the Tsar!
Swear your allegiance to your lawful master;
Be humbled now, and send with no delay   30
An embassy to pay Dimítry homage:
Archbishop, boyars, delegates and scribes
Will bow in their obeisance to the Tsar.

(*He leaves.*)
(*A murmur runs through the crowd.*)

A VOICE FROM THE CROWD
What can we say? The boyar spoke the truth.
Long live Dimítry, Moscow's rightful Tsar.   35

A PEASANT (*on the platform*)
Let's go! The Kremlin palace, brothers, quick!
Come on! We'll put Borís's whelp in chains!

THE PEOPLE
Let's take him! Drown the pup! Long live Dimítry!
And death to all the house of Godunóv!

SCENE 23

The Kremlin. The apartments of Borís

(*A guard on the porch;* FEÓDOR *at a window.*)

A BEGGAR Alms for the poor... for the love of Christ!

GUARD Get out of here. No one can speak with the prisoners.

FEÓDOR Go along, old man; I'm poorer than you; you're free.

(KSENIA, *in a veil, also appears at the window.*)

ONE OF THE PEOPLE Brother and sister! Poor children, like birds in a cage. 5

ANOTHER Don't waste your pity on them—accursèd brood!

FIRST MAN The father was the villain; the young ones aren't to blame.

ANOTHER The apple doesn't fall far from the tree.

KSENIA My brother, I hear the boyars coming. 10

FEÓDOR I see Golítsyn and Mosálsky. The others I don't know.

KSENIA Oh, brother, I'm so full of fear!

(GOLÍTSYN, MOSÁLSKY, MOLCHÁNOV *and* SHEREFEDÍNOV *move through the crowd, three of the Tsar's guard behind them.*)

THE CROWD Make way, make way. Here come the boyars.

(*They enter the building.*)

ONE OF THE PEOPLE What have they come for? 15

ANOTHER No doubt to take Feódor Godunóv to swear the oath.

A THIRD You think so?... You hear that noise inside! That uproar... they're struggling...

THE PEOPLE Hear that? A scream! That's a woman's voice...   20
Let's go in!... The doors are locked... The shrieking stopped.

(*The doors open.* MOSÁLSKY *steps out on the landing.*)

MOSÁLSKY People! Maria Godunóva and her son Feódor have
taken poison. We have seen their dead corpses. (*The people
fall mute in horror.*) Why don't you speak? Let's hear your
cry: Long live the Tsar, Dimítry Ivánovich!   25

The PEOPLE *are silent.*

A SCENE FROM FAUST

A seacoast

FAUST *and* MEPHISTOPHELES

FAUST
  Demon, I'm bored.

MEPHISTO   What of it, Faust?
  For that's the lot you've been assigned,
  And none beyond his lot may go.
  All sentient creatures suffer so:
  The idle and the active mind;   5
  Believer and the undeceived;
  Both he who never joy did find,
  And he who too much joy received;
  Thus all must yawn and live their fates—
  All those the yawning grave awaits.   10
  You, too, must yawn.

FAUST   An arid jest!
  But can you not at least provide
  Distraction then?

MEPHISTO   Be satisfied
  With reason's proof and take your rest.
  Within your book inscribe it deep: 15
  Fastidium est quies—or—
  Ennui allows the soul to sleep.
  A master I of psychic lore!...
  But when were you not bored, alas?
  Consider well. Was it back then,   20
  When Virgil made you doze in class
  And canings woke you up again?
  Or back when you with roses crowned
  Compliant maidens of delight
  And in abandoned revels drowned   25
  The ardours of the drunken night?

Or back when you were so immersed
In all those noble dreams you nursed,
In learning's dark, unfathomed well?
But then, as I recall, from hell   30
You chose at last to summon me,
A harlequin to chase ennui.
A petty fiend, by might and main
I did my best to entertain;
I brought you sprites, and witches, too—   35
With what result? Just much ado.
You wanted glory—and achieved it,
You wanted love—and you received it.
You took from life the gifts she bore,
But were you happy?

FAUST   Speak no more!   40
You aggravate my secret woe.
Great knowledge proves in life a blight—
I curse its false, deceptive light;
And as for glory's passing glow,
It never stays. The world's respect   45
Is meaningless and vain... and yet,
There is one single good—the union
Of kindred souls...

MEPHISTO   And first communion,
As you'll agree! But might one know
Just who it is you treasure so,   50
Not Gretchen, pray?

FAUST   O wondrous dream!
O purest, brightest flame of love!
Oh there, beside the burbling stream,
The shady rustling trees above—
Upon her lovely breast to dream,   55
In languor once my head I lay
And savoured joy...

MEPHISTO   You're so extreme!
   Good lord, you're raving, Faust, I'd say.
   With this enticing recollection
   You'll fall into deceit's embrace.   60
   For was it not by my direction
   That you were granted beauty's grace?
   Was it not I in darkest night
   Who brought her there to be with you?
   I had my lonely pleasures, too,   65
   In relishing my labour's might,
   And still recall that scene I do.
   But as your lady's rapture grew,
   And she succumbed to passion's throes,
   I saw that you, my restless friend,   70
   Were lost in contemplation's woes.
   (And you and I well comprehend
   That boredom thrives on contemplation.)
   And do you know, my pensive friend,
   Just what you thought on that occasion,   75
   A time when no one turns to thought?
   Shall I be frank?

FAUST   Well, tell me, what?

MEPHISTO
   You thought: how avidly, my dove,
   Did I pursue you with desire!
   How cunningly with dreams of love   80
   Did I her maiden heart inspire!
   She gave herself, so pure and fair,
   To passions that she never sought...
   Yet why is now my spirit fraught
   With dreadful boredom and despair?   85
   Once having satisfied my lust,
   I gaze upon my victim's face
   With irrepressible disgust:
   Just so a foolish rogue, in haste,
   Miscalculates and kills in vain,   90

Then heaps abuse upon the head
Of some poor pauper that he's slain.
Just so corruption, quickly fed
And sated with its purchased bliss,
Regards in fear the black abyss...   95
And with these thoughts upon your plight,
You made a single calculation...

FAUST

Avaunt thee, creature of damnation!
Remove thy figure from my sight!

MEPHISTO

If that's your wish. But charge me first.   100
Without assignment, as you know,
I dare not from your presence go;
Such waste of time would leave me cursed.

FAUST

What's that I see, that patch of white?

MEPHISTO

A triple-masted Spanish barque,   105
Hell-bent for Holland ere the dark.
Aboard—three hundred rogues outright,
Two monkeys, seven pots of gold,
Rich chocolate in the cargo hold,
And one quite modish illness, too: 110
The one just lately given you.

FAUST

Go drown them all.

MEPHISTO

                    At once.

                (He disappears.)

THE LITTLE TRAGEDIES

I

THE MISERLY KNIGHT

Scenes from Shenstone's Tragicomedy,
The Covetous Knight

SCENE I

A tower

ALBERT *and* JEAN

ALBERT
    Whatever be the cost, I must appear
    At tournament. Let's see my helmet, Jean.

            (JEAN *brings him his helmet*.)

    It's pierced all through, quite useless. Not a chance
    Of wearing it. I'll needs obtain another.
    A mighty stroke! That cursèd Count Delorge!   5

JEAN
    But you requited him right well, my lord.
    And after you had dropped him from his horse,
    He lay like death all day and night—I doubt
    He's well.

ALBERT   And yet he suffered no great loss;
    His fine Venetian breastplate's still intact;   10
    His breast's his own—it cost him not a farthing,
    Nor will he need to buy himself another.
    I should have stripped his helmet where he lay!
    And would have done, had I not been ashamed
    Before the Duke and ladies. Cursèd Count!   15
    Far better had he gored my skull instead.
    I need new raiment too. Last time the knights
    Were all in satin and in velvet clad;
    While I alone, among the ducal guests,
    Sat clothed in coat-of-mail. I made excuse,   20
    By claiming that I'd happened there by chance.
    But what shall I say now? This wretched state!
    How poverty humiliates the heart!
    When that Delorge with his full-weighted lance

Did run my helmet through and gallop past,   25
And I, with all-uncovered head, did spur
My steed Emir and like a whirlwind rushed
Upon the Count and hurled him like a page
Full twenty steps; when all the ladies then
Uprose them from their chairs; when fair Clotilda,   30
Her eyelids closed, unknowingly cried out,
And all the heralds praised my mighty blow—
Oh, none of them had inkling of the cause,
The reason for my courage and my strength!
I went berserk to see my helmet crushed—   35
The parent to my deed was paltry meanness.
Oh yes, that foul disease attaches quick
When one resides beneath my father's roof!
How fares my poor Emir?

JEAN   Still lame, I fear.
You'll not be riding him for some good time.   40

ALBERT

There's nothing to be done; I'll buy the bay.
The asking price, at least, is nothing much.

JEAN

Not much, perhaps, but money have we none.

ALBERT

What says that worthless scoundrel Solomon?

JEAN

He says that he no longer can afford   45
To lend you any funds without a pledge.

ALBERT

A pledge! And what am I to pledge, the devil?

JEAN

I told him that.

ALBERT   What then?

JEAN   He groaned and shrugged.

ALBERT
  You should have told him that my father's rich,
  And like a Jew himself; that soon or late   50
  His wealth will pass to me.

JEAN   I told him so.

ALBERT
  And then?

JEAN   He shrugged and groaned.

ALBERT   What wretched luck!

JEAN
  He said he'd come himself.

ALBERT   Thank God for that.
  I'll have a ransom ere I let him go.

(*A knock at the door.*)

  Who's there?

(*A* JEW *enters.*)

JEW   Your humble servant.

ALBERT   Ah, my friend!   55
  Accursèd Jew, most worthy Solomon,
  Come in, come in! What's this they tell me, friend:
  That you mistrust a debt?

JEW   Oh, noble knight,
  I swear to you... I'd gladly... but I can't.
  I have no funds. I've made myself a bankrupt   60
  By slavishly assisting all you knights.
  For no one pays me back. I came to ask
  If you could pay at least some part...

ALBERT   You thief!
  If I myself had funds, do you believe
  I'd have the slightest intercourse with you?   65

Be not so obdurate, friend Solomon,
Release your gold. A hundred you can spare.
I'll have you searched.

JEW   A hundred, did you say!
Oh, when have I had such a sum!

ALBERT   Take care...
You ought to be ashamed that you refuse   70
To aid a friend.

JEW   I swear to you...

ALBERT   Enough.
You want a pledge? What sort of rant is this!
What kind of pledge? A boar-skin, would you say?
Had I the merest trifle I could pledge,
I'd sold it long ere this. A knight's good word   75
Is not enough for you, you dog?

JEW   Your word,
While you're alive, is worth a great, great deal.
It's like a talisman that can unlock,
For you, the chests of all the Flemish rich.
But if you then transfer that word to me,   80
A wretched Jew, and if you chance to die
(Which God forbid!), then in these hands of mine,
'Twould be no use... or like a key that fits
Some casket at the bottom of the sea.

ALBERT
You think it true, my father will outlive me?   85

JEW
Who knows? Our days are reckoned not by us;
The youth who bloomed last night today lies dead,
And four old men, on bent and burdened shoulders,
Now bear him in his coffin to the grave.
The Baron's hale. God will—he'll live for ten,   90
For twenty, twenty-five... for thirty years.

ALBERT

    You lie, you wretched dog: in thirty years—
    I'll be nigh fifty, Jew! What earthly good
    Will money do me then?

JEW   What good, you ask?

    Why, money serves us well at any age;   95
    But youth, in wealth, seeks nothing more than servants
    And, pitiless, dispatches them all round.
    Old age, in wealth, sees good and worthy friends
    And guards them like the apple of his eye.

ALBERT

    My father neither friends nor servants sees;   100
    He only sees the master whom he serves.
    And how he serves! Like some Egyptian slave
    Or chainèd dog. In his unheated kennel
    He lives on water and on crusts of bread;
    He never sleeps, but runs about and howls—   105
    While all his gold rests peacefully in chests.
    Be silent, Jew! The day will surely come
    When it will rest no more, but service me.

JEW

    The funeral of the Baron will unleash
    A great deal more of money than of tears.   110
    God grant you your inheritance ere long.

ALBERT

    Amen!

JEW   Perhaps...

ALBERT   What now?

JEW   I had a thought,

    That maybe there's a way...

ALBERT   What way?

JEW   Well then—

    I have a friend, a little agèd fellow,

A Jew, a poor apothecary...

ALBERT   Ha!   115
A usurer like you. Or is he honest?

JEW
No, knight, Tobias deals a different trade.
He mixes potions... and his drops, in truth,
Work wondrous well.

ALBERT   And what are they to me?

JEW
Three drops is all—into a glass of water;   120
They have no taste, no colour do they show;
And he who drinks will have no writhing gut,
No nausea, no pain... and yet will die.

ALBERT
Your agèd friend in poison trades.

JEW   Ah, yes,
In poison.

ALBERT   So? Instead of lending cash,   125
You offer me two hundred venomed vials,
A vial for a coin? Is that your game?

JEW
You choose to laugh at me, my noble knight—
But no, I thought... perhaps that you... I thought...
The Baron's time to die might well have come.   130

ALBERT
What's that!... a son... give poison to his father!
Arrest him, Jean! How dare you think that I...
Do you not know, you Jewish thing, you dog,
You serpent, you! that I can hang you now
Upon these gateposts here!

JEW   I did you wrong!   135
Have mercy, I but jested.

ALBERT   Jean, the rope!

JEW

A jest... a jest... I have the money... here!

ALBERT

Away, you dog!

(*The* JEW *leaves.*)

                    Thus low have I been brought
By this my father's greed! See what the Jew
Has dared suggest! Bring me a glass of wine...   140
I'm all distraught... And yet... the money, Jean—
I need it! Follow that accursèd Jew
And take his gold away. And bring me then
A pot of ink. I'll give the wretched rogue
A full receipt. But don't admit the man,   145
That Judas soul... But stay you, Jean... I fear
His gold will reek of poison evermore,
As did that silver of his ancestor...
I asked for wine.

JEAN   We haven't, sir, alas,
A drop of wine.

ALBERT   But what about the crate   150
That Raymond sent me, as a gift, from Spain?

JEAN

Just yesterday I took the ailing smith
Our final bottle.

ALBERT   Yes, I do recall...
Well, pour me water then. This cursèd life!
The die is cast. I'll get me to the Duke   155
And seek redress: let father be compelled
To treat me as a son... and not a mouse
Begotten in a cellar.

SCENE II

A cellar vault

BARON
    The way a youthful rake awaits a tryst
    With some licentious harlot or, perhaps,
    Some foolish girl that he's seduced, so I
    All day have marked the time till I might come
    Down to my secret vault and trusty chests.   5
    O happy day! This evening can I pour
    In coffer number six (as yet unfilled)
    Another gathered handful of my gold.
    Not much, perhaps, but by such tiny drops
    Do mighty treasures grow. I read somewhere   10
    That once a king commanded all his troops
    To gather dirt by handfuls in a heap,
    And thus, in time, a mighty hill arose—
    And from that summit could the king with joy
    Survey his valleys, decked in gleaming tents,   15
    And watch his great armada ply the sea.
    Thus I, by offering in tiny bits
    My customary tribute to this vault,
    Have raised my hill as well—and from its height
    I too survey the reach of my domain.   20
    And who shall set its bounds? Like some great demon,
    From here I can control and rule the world.
    I need but wish—and palaces will rise;
    And in my splendid gardens will appear
    A throng of nymphs to caper and to sport;   25
    The muses too will offer me their tribute,
    And freedom-loving genius be my slave;
    And virtue too, and unremitting labour,
    Will humbly wait on me for their reward.
    I need but whistle low—and, bowing, scraping,   30
    Blood-spattered villainy itself will crawl

To lick my hand and look into my eyes
To read therein the sign of my desire.
All things submit to me, and I—to none;
I stand above all longings and all cares;   35
I know my might, and in this knowledge find
Enough reward...

(He looks at his gold.)

It hardly seems like much,
But oh what human woes, what bitter tears,
Deceptions, orisons, and imprecations
This heavy-weighted gold is token of!   40
I have an old doubloon... it's this one here;
Some widow brought it just this morn, but first
She knelt for half the day outside my window,
Three children at her side, and wailed aloud.
It rained and rained, then stopped, then rained again,   45
And still that hypocrite stayed on; I might
Have driven her away, but something whispered
That she had come to pay her husband's debt,
Afraid that on the morrow she'd be jailed.
And this one here was brought me by Thibault—   50
A lazy cheat who got it God knows where!
He lifted it, no doubt; or else outside,
Upon the highroad, late at night, in woods...
Ah yes! If all the tears, the blood and sweat
That men have shed for such a hoard as this   55
Should suddenly gush forth from out the earth,
There'd be a second flood!—and I'd be drowned
Inside my trusty vaults. But now it's time.

(He starts to unlock the chest.)

Each time I come to open up a chest,
I fall into a fever and I shudder.   60
It isn't fear (for whom have I to dread?
I have my sabre by; its trusty steel
Will answer for my gold), but all the same

Some strange and eerie feeling grips my heart...
Physicians claim that there are certain men   65
Who find a pleasure in the act of murder.
When I insert my key inside the lock,
I feel what murderers themselves must feel
As they plunge dagger into flesh: Excitement...
And horror all at once.

(He opens the chest.)

My ecstasy!   70

(He slowly pours in his coins.)

You're home! You've roamed the world quite long enough
In service to the needs and lusts of men.
Sleep well in here—the sleep of peace and power,
The sleep the gods in deepest heaven sleep...
I will arrange tonight a solemn feast: 75
Before each chest I'll light a candlestick,
And all of them I'll open wide, and I
Will gaze in rapture at my dazzling hoard.

*(He lights the candles and, one after the other,
opens all the chests.)*

I rule the world!... What magical refulgence!
And all this mighty realm submits to me;   80
My bliss is here, my honour and my glory!
I rule the world!... But who, when I have gone,
Will reign in this domain? My wretched heir!
A raving madman and a spendthrift youth,
The comrade of licentious debauchees!   85
Before I'm cold, he'll come! He'll hurry down,
With all his crew of greedy sycophants,
To enter these serene and silent vaults.
He'll rob my corpse and, when he has the keys,
He'll cackle as he opens all the chests.   90
And all my treasured gold will quickly flow
To pockets satin-lined and full of holes.

He'll desecrate and smash these hallowed vessels,
He'll feed the regal balm to dirt and dust—
He'll squander all!... And by what proper right?!   95
Have I, indeed, attained all this by nought?
Or through a game, as if I were a gambler
Who rattles dice and rakes the booty in?
Who knows how many bitter deprivations,
How many bridled passions, heavy thoughts,   100
Unceasing cares, and sleepless nights I've paid?
Or will my callous son assert aloud
That my poor heart was all o'ergrown with moss,
That never did I know immortal longings,
That conscience never gnawed me, mighty conscience,   105
The sharp-clawed beast that rakes the heart; O conscience,
That uninvited guest, that dull companion,
That churlish creditor, that horrid witch,
Upon whose call the moon grows dark, and tombs
Convulse... and send their dead to roam abroad?...   110
No! Suffer first! and earn the wealth you crave,
And then we'll see, if you'd allow some wretch
To squander all the treasure got by blood.
If only I could hide this sacred vault
From worthless eyes! If only from the grave   115
I might return and, like a watchful shade,
Secure my chests and from all living souls
Protect my treasured gold, as I do now!...

SCENE III

At the Palace

ALBERT *and the* DUKE

ALBERT

Believe me, sovereign liege, I've long endured
The shame of bitter want. Were not my plight
extreme indeed, you had not heard my plaint.

DUKE

I well believe you, sir: a noble knight,
A man like you, would not accuse his father   5
Except in deep distress. Such knaves are few...
So rest your mind; I shall appeal, myself,
In private, gently, to your father's heart.
I wait him now. It's long since last we met.
He was my grandsire's friend. I well recall—   10
When I was still a boy, your father oft
Would seat me on his stallion and, in jest,
Would place his heavy helm upon my head,
As if it were a bell.

               (*He looks out of the window.*)

               Who comes here now?
Your father?

ALBERT   He, my liege.

DUKE   Then get you hence.   15
I'll summon you when all's arranged.

          (ALBERT *leaves, the* BARON *enters.*)

                    Well, Baron,
I'm pleased to see you, and so hale and hearty.

BARON

I'm overjoyed, my liege, to have the strength
To come to court once more, at your command.

DUKE

    It's been some time since last we parted, Baron.   20
    Do you remember me?

BARON   Remember, lord?

    I see you even now as once you were—
    A lively boy. The great deceasèd Duke
    Would say: 'Well, Philip, friend' (he called me that;
    'Twas always 'Philip' then), 'what say you, eh?   25
    In twenty years or so, both you and I
    Will be but dotards in this stripling's eyes...'
    In yours, that is to say.

DUKE   Well, let's renew

    Our friendship now. You've quite forgot my court.

BARON

    I've grown too old, my liege. And here at court   30
    What use am I? You're young and still delight
    In tournaments and festive rounds. But I
    Am little fit for such pursuits. If God
    Should send us war, then I'd remain prepared
    To mount, if groaningly, my horse once more;   35
    I'd find the strength, although my hand might tremble,
    To draw my ancient sword in your behalf.

DUKE

    Your valour, Baron, is well known to us;
    You were my grandsire's friend; my father too
    Respected you. And I have ever found you   40
    A brave and worthy knight... But come, we'll sit.
    You've children, Baron, yes?

BARON   An only son.

DUKE

    Why is it that he hides from our regard?
    The court for you is dull, but for your son
    Both age and rank do call him to our side.   45

BARON
    My son dislikes the bustling, courtly life.
    He has a shy and gloomy cast of mind—
    All round the castle wood he ever roams,
    As if he were a fawn.

DUKE   It bodes no good
    To shun the light. We'll soon accustom him   50
    To festive rounds, to tournaments and balls.
    Assign him here to us, and do bestow
    A maintenance upon him due his rank.
    I see you frown—your journey, I much fear,
    Has laid you low.

BARON   I am not weary, liege,   55
    But you have much confused me. I would fain
    Not make confession to Your Grace... but now,
    You force me to be frank about my son,
    To tell you what I'd rather keep well hid.
    My sovereign liege: my son, alas, deserves   60
    No mark of your good favour or regard.
    He wastes away his youth in brute excess,
    In basest vice...

DUKE   The cause may be, good Baron,
    That he's too much alone. Great solitude
    And idleness prove ruinous to youth.   65
    Appoint him then to us, and he'll forget
    Those habits that forsakenness doth breed.

BARON
    Forgive me, sovereign liege, but I protest;
    I cannot give consent to such a course.

DUKE
    But, Baron, why?

BARON   Release a poor old man...   70

DUKE
I must insist, old friend, that you reveal
The cause of your refusal.

BARON   Anger, liege,
Against my son.

DUKE   For what?

BARON   A wicked crime.

DUKE
But tell me, knight, in what does it consist?

BARON
Release me, Duke, I pray.

DUKE   'Tis passing strange...   75
Or feel you shame on his account?

BARON   Yes... shame...

DUKE
What was it, though, he did?

BARON   He tried... he sought...
To murder me.

DUKE   To murder you! See here,
I'll have the wretched villain bound to court.

BARON
I cannot offer proof, although I know   80
He greatly thirsts indeed to see me dead;
And well I know that he had dark intent
To...

DUKE What?

BARON   To rob me.

                (ALBERT *rushes into the room.*)

ALBERT   Baron, that's a lie!

DUKE (*to the son*)
　　How dare you, sir!...

BARON　　　　　　　You here! And dare to speak,
　　To hurl at me, your father, such a word!...　　　　　85
　　To say—I lie! Before our noble Duke!...
　　To me... or am I knight no more!

ALBERT　　　　　　　　You lie!

BARON
　　O God of justice, sound thy thunder now!
　　Pick up my gauntlet—let the sword decide!

　　　　(*He throws down his glove, his son promptly picks it up.*)

ALBERT
　　My gratitude. Your first paternal gift.　　　　　　90

DUKE
　　What's this I see? Before my very eyes?
　　A son takes up an agèd father's dare!
　　O woeful times are these that I should wear
　　The ducal crown! Be silent, madman, you.
　　And you, you tiger cub, enough.

　　　　　　　　　(*to the son.*)

　　　　　　　　　Have done;　　　　　　95
　　Relinquish me that glove.

　　　　　　　(*He takes it away.*)

ALBERT (*aside*)　　　　A pity that.

DUKE
　　He's marked it with his claws! A monstrous son!
　　Begone; and keep thee, sirrah, from my sight,
　　Until such time as I, upon the need,
　　May summon you.

　　　　　　　(ALBERT *leaves.*)

And you, unhappy wretch,   100
Have you no shame?...

BARON   Forgive me, noble liege...
I feel unwell... my knees have turned to water...
I'm choking!... choking!... air!... the keys? The keys!
I want my keys!...

DUKE   He's dead. O God in heaven!
What dreadful times are these, what dreadful hearts!   105

II

MOZART AND SALIERI

SCENE I

A room

SALIERI

Men say, there is no justice here on earth.
I say, there's none on high as well. To me
This seems as clear as any simple scale.
I came into this world in love with art;
While still a boy I listened and was thrilled   5
When in our ancient church the organ sang,
And deep within my soul the music swelled,
As sweet unbidden tears poured down my cheeks.
I early turned away from idle pleasures;
All studies far from music I despised;   10
And, scorning them with chill and stubborn pride,
In music I invested all my hopes.
First steps to any goal are always hard,
And arduous and long the path ahead.
But all my early trials I o'ercame,   15
And craft I made the basis of my art.
A craftsman I became: I made my fingers
The servants who would race to do my will;
My ear I trained: subduing potent sounds,
I disassembled music like a corpse,   20
Put harmony to algebraic test,
And only then, well steeped in practised craft,
Did I embrace the lure of true creation.
I set to work... but secretly, alone,
Not daring yet to dream of future fame;   25
Oh, many times, inside my silent cell,
Not having slept or fed for days on end,
And having tasted inspiration's tears,
I burnt my work... and watched, aloof and cold,
My thoughts and sounds, those children of my soul,   30
Take flame... and vanish in a wisp of smoke.

Oh, more than this! When mighty Gluck* appeared
And showed the world the secrets he had found
(Great captivating harmonies of sound),
Did I not then abandon all I knew,   35
All things I'd loved and ardently believed,
To follow bravely on the track he laid,
Without complaint, like one who'd lost his way
And from some fellow traveller learned the path?
Through constancy of deep intense endeavour,   40
In time I proved successful and attained
The limitless and lofty realms of art;
And fame at last presented me its kiss.
My work had found a place in people's hearts,
And, happy, I enjoyed with deep content   45
My labour, my success, my growing fame.
I prized no less the triumphs of my friends,
My fellow craftsmen in this wondrous art.
And never did I feel a jealous pang!
Not even when Piccinni* with his charm   50
Enraptured fickle Paris for a time,
Not even when I heard with bated breath
The overture from *Iphigenia*￼ soar.
And who would dare to say that proud Salieri
Could ever, like a snake, with envy crawl?   55
That, trampled underfoot, in mortal pain,
He'd gnaw with helpless rage the dirt and dust?
No man would dare! But I myself now say:
Salieri crawls! Yes, I, the great Salieri,
Am tortured and consumed by envy's sting.   60
O Heaven! Where is justice to be found?!
When genius, that immortal sacred gift
Is granted not to love and self-denial,
To labour and to striving and to prayer—
But casts its light upon a madman's head,   65
A foolish idler's brow?... O Mozart, Mozart!

(MOZART *enters.*)

MOZART
    Aha! You've seen me then! And here I'd hoped
    To treat you to an unexpected jest.

SALIERI
    How long have you been here!

MOZART   I came just now.
    I'd started out to show you my new piece;   70
    And on the way, while passing by the inn,
    I heard a violin... Oh, good Salieri!
    In all your days you've never heard, I swear,
    A droller sound... A blind old fiddler there
    Was scraping out '*Voi che sapete*'.* Bliss!   75
    I couldn't wait—and brought the fellow here
    To treat you to the pleasure of his art.
    Come in!

        (*A blind old man with a violin enters.*)

MOZART   A bit of Mozart, if you will!

    (*The old man plays an aria from* Don Giovanni.
        MOZART *roars with laughter.*)

SALIERI
    And you can laugh at this?

MOZART   Salieri, come!
    Are you not laughing too, my friend?

SALIERI   Oh, no!   80
    I cannot laugh—when some benighted hack
    Besmirches Raphael and his Madonna;
    I cannot laugh—when some repellent clown
    With parody dishonours Alighieri.
    Begone, old man.

MOZART   Here wait... take this, my friend,   85
    And drink my health.

        (*The old man leaves.*)

MOZART   I see, my good Salieri,
   You're out of sorts today. I'll call again
   Some other time.

SALIERI   What was it that you brought me?

MOZART
   Indeed, it's nothing much. For some nights past,
   As sleeplessness tormented me again,   90
   A phrase or two kept running through my mind.
   I wrote them down this morning—and I'd come
   To ask for your opinion... but I see...
   You're hardly in the mood.

SALIERI   Oh, Mozart, Mozart!
   Not in the mood for you? Oh, come, sit down,   95
   I'll hear you play.

MOZART (*at the fortepiano*)
                Now picture... let me see?...
   Well... *me*, let's say—a somewhat younger version,
   In love—not overmuch, but slightly so;
   I'm with a lady... or a friend... say *you*;
   I'm cheerful... then... some vision from the grave...   100
   A darkness comes... or something of the kind...
   Now listen...

                (*He plays.*)

SALIERI   You were bringing *this* to me!
   And yet could loiter at a wretched inn
   To hear some blind old fiddler play! O God!
   Oh, Mozart, you're unworthy of yourself.   105

MOZART
   You think it good?

SALIERI   What richness and what depth!
   What boldness of design and grace of form!
   You, Mozart, are a god and know it not.
   But I, I know.

MOZART   You do? Well, maybe so...
But now this little god is rather famished.   110

SALIERI

I tell you what: let's go and dine together,
The Tavern at the Golden Lion Inn.

MOZART

How nice. But let me first drop in at home
To tell my wife, I won't be there for supper.

(MOZART *leaves*.)

SALIERI

I'll meet you there. I'll wait. Don't fail me, Mozart.   115
No more! No more can I resist my fate:
This night shall his undoing bring... and I
Must be the cause! Or else we all are lost!
Not I alone, with my dim spot of fame,
But all who worship and who serve our art.   120
What good if Mozart live? Or if indeed
He soar to such a height as none before?
Will he, by this, exalt the realm of art?
Not so! For fall it must when he departs,
And no successor will he leave behind.   125
What profit then his life? Like some great angel
He brought immortal music from the skies
To stir within poor creatures of the dust
Unwingèd dreams... and then—to fly away!
Go now, Mozart! You are too good for earth.   130
This poison was a gift from my Isora.
I've had it with me now for eighteen years;
How often since she left have I known pain;
How often have my heedless foe and I
Shared meals together at a single board;   135
Yet never have I yielded to temptation;
No cowardice has kept me from the deed,
Nor is it that I take offences lightly,
Nor do I hold for life a high regard.

Yet I delayed. Some last resolve I lacked.   140
Whenever dreams of death beset my soul,
I thought upon the gifts that life might bring:
Of joys unknown, abandoned ere they came;
Of night's creative bliss, and inspiration;
Of how another Haydn might compose   145
Great masterworks—whose depths I then could plumb...
And while I've feasted with my hateful guest,
I've often thought that one day I would meet
My mortal foe; or else some rank offence
Would fall upon my head from haughty heights—   150
And then Isora's gift would do its work.
And I was right! The enemy I sought
Is in my hands at last! Another Haydn—
Who ravished me with ecstasies of sound!
The time has come! O thou prophetic gift,   155
Get thee tonight... into friendship's cup!

SCENE II

A private room at an inn; a piano

MOZART *and* SALIERI *at a table*

SALIERI
You seem in blackish mood tonight?

MOZART   Not so.

SALIERI
But something, Mozart, troubles you, I fear.
A splendid meal... a wine beyond compare,
Yet you sit dark and mute.

MOZART   I must confess,
My Requiem is on my mind.

SALIERI   Aha!   5
A requiem! How long have you been working?

MOZART
For three whole weeks. The circumstance was strange...
I haven't told you?

SALIERI   No.

MOZART   I'll tell you now:
About three weeks ago I came home late,
And learned that, while I'd been away that evening,   10
A man had called. I don't know why myself,
But all that night I wondered who he was,
And why he'd come. Next day he reappeared,
But found me once again away from home.
Next afternoon, while romping with my son   15
About the floor, I heard my name called out.
I went below. A man, all dressed in black,
With solemn bow, commissioned from my hand
A requiem, and disappeared. At once

I set to work—but ever since that day,   20
My visitor in black has not returned.
Which suits me fine, for though my work is done,
I'm loath to give it up. And yet...

SALIERI   Go on.

MOZART

I'm quite ashamed to tell you this...

SALIERI   What is it?

MOZART

All day and night, my caller dressed in black   25
Looms heavy in my mind and haunts my peace.
He follows like a shadow where I go,
And even now, I sense him near... a third...
Who dines with us tonight.

SALIERI   What childish fears!
Dispel such empty thoughts. Old Beaumarchais   30
Quite often used to tell me: 'Good Salieri,
Whenever morbid thoughts invade your mind,
Uncork a sparkling bottle of champagne,
Or else, go read my *Figaro* again.'

MOZART

Yes, you and Beaumarchais were friends, I know;   35
You put his play *Tarare** into song...
A splendid thing. There's one motif of yours
I love to sing... when in a happy mood...
La-la la-la... But is it true, Salieri,
That Beaumarchais gave poison to a friend?   40

SALIERI

I doubt it's true—he seemed too droll a man
For such a crafty deed.

MOZART   He was a genius,
Like you and me. And villainy and genius,
As you'll agree, my friend, sit ill together.

SALIERI
    You think so?

                (*He pours the poison into* MOZART'*s drink.*)

            Mozart, have a drink.

MOZART   Your health,   45
    Good friend, and to the deep and lasting bonds
    That link forever Mozart and Salieri,
    Two sons of blessèd harmony.

                        (*He drinks.*)

SALIERI   No, wait!
    You've drunk it down!... And couldn't wait for me?

MOZART (*throwing his napkin onto the table*)
    I've had enough.

                    (*He goes to the fortepiano.*)

                    I'll play you now, Salieri,   50
    My Requiem.

                        (*He plays.*)

            You weep?

SALIERI   I've never shed
    Such tears before: I feel both pain and joy,
    As if I'd just fulfilled some heavy debt,
    As if a healing knife had just cut off
    An aching limb! Dear Mozart, pay no mind   55
    To these my tears. Don't stop, play on... play on
    And fill my soul once more with magic sound...

MOZART
    If only all could feel as you, Salieri,
    The power of the music! Ah... but then,
    The world itself would crumble into dust,   60
    For all would seek the freedom to create,
    And none would then attend to petty needs.

We are but few... a happy, chosen few,
Who hold in scorn the vulgar path of use,
Who worship only beauty... nothing else.   65
Is that not so? But here... I feel unwell,
Some heaviness upon me sits. I'll sleep.
Good night.

SALIERI   Farewell, my friend.

                            (*Alone*.)

                        You'll fall asleep
Forever, Mozart! But could he be right...
Am I no genius? 'Villainy and genius   70
Sit ill together.' Surely this is wrong:
Take Michelangelo? Or is it only
A tale the dull and witless tell—and he,
The Vatican's creator, was no murderer?

III

THE STONE GUEST

LEPORELLO: O statua gentilissima
Del gran' Commendatore!...
...Ah, Padrone!

Don Giovanni

SCENE I

DON JUAN *and* LEPORELLO

DON JUAN
> We'll wait for nightfall here. And so at last
> We've reached the very gates of old Madrid!
> I'll soon be racing down familiar streets,
> My face behind a cloak, my hat pulled down.
> What think you, am I well disguised or no?   5

LEPORELLO
> Oh, surely none will recognize Don Juan!
> One sees such figures all about!

DON JUAN   You laugh?
> But who would know it's I?

LEPORELLO   Why, any watchman,
> Or gypsy that you meet, or drunken fiddler,
> Or one like you—some brazen cavalier,   10
> With sword beneath his cloak and black as night.

DON JUAN
> What matter then if I be seen? Of course,
> The King himself I'd best avoid. But come,
> I fear no other man in all Madrid.

LEPORELLO
> By morning, though, the King will surely learn   15
> That once again Don Juan is in Madrid,
> Returned from banishment without permission.
> What then will be your fate?

DON JUAN   He'll send me back.
> I greatly doubt, old man, he'll take my head,
> For after all, I'm guilty of no treason.   20
> The King dispatched me hence with kind intent,

To gain me safety from the vengeful kin
Of one I killed...

LEPORELLO   Indeed he did! Just so!
And safe you should have stayed and not returned.

DON JUAN
Your humble servant! God, I all but died   25
Of boredom there. I never saw such folk!
And what a land! The sky... a pall of smoke.
Their women... ha! Why, I would never trade,
I'll have you know, my foolish Leporello,
The lowest peasant girl in Andalusia   30
For all their proudest beauties, I do swear.
At first I rather liked them, I'll admit—
Their deep blue eyes, the whiteness of their skin,
Their modest ways... and most of all, their novelty;
But thank the Lord, I quickly saw the light   35
And saved myself from falling in their grasp.
They have no spark, they're all but waxen dolls;
While women here!... But look you, Leporello,
We've seen this place before; it seems familiar.

LEPORELLO
It is. The convent of Saint Anthony.   40
You used to come here late at night, while I...
I watched the horses in this very grove,
A wretched task, I have to say. But you,
You had a grand old time... far more than I,
As I can well attest.

DON JUAN (*pensively*)
                    My poor Inéz!   45
She's dead and gone! And how I loved her then!

LEPORELLO
Inéz... the dark-eyed one... Oh, I recall!
Three months or so you courted her in vain,
Then won her, with the devil's help, at last.

DON JUAN

   July it was... at night. I always found   50
   A strange attraction in her mournful eyes
   And pallid lips. How strange it is, how strange.
   You never thought her beautiful, I know,
   And yes, it's true—she wasn't what you'd call
   A dazzling beauty. But those eyes of hers,   55
   Those eyes... her searching look. I've never known
   So beautiful a gaze. And then her voice—
   As soft and weak as some poor invalid's...
   Her husband was a hard and vicious brute,
   As I soon after learned... My poor Inéz!...   60

LEPORELLO

   No matter though, for others followed.

DON JUAN   True.

LEPORELLO

   And while we live, still others will there be.

DON JUAN

   Indeed.

LEPORELLO

       Which lady now in all Madrid
   Do we intend to seek?

DON JUAN   Why, Laura, fool!
   I'm off to her this very night.

LEPORELLO   Of course.   65

DON JUAN

   I'll straightway to her room—and if, perchance,
   A man is there, I'll speed him out the window.

LEPORELLO

   Quite so. And see how greatly cheered we are.
   The dead need not disturb us overlong.
   But someone comes.

            (A MONK *enters.)*

MONK   She'll be here any moment.   70
  And who are you? From Dona Anna's house?

LEPORELLO
  Why, no, we're honest gentlemen ourselves,
  Just come to see the sights.

DON JUAN   And you're expecting?

MONK
  The pious Dona Anna shortly comes
  To look upon her husband's grave.

DON JUAN   De Solva?   75
  The slain Commander's widow, Dona Anna?
  Though slain by whom I can't recall.

MONK   That foul,
  Depraved, and godless reprobate, Don Juan.

LEPORELLO
  Aha! The reputation of Don Juan
  Has penetrated even convent walls,   80
  And anchorites now sing his praises, too.

MONK
  You know the man?

LEPORELLO   Oh not at all, not we.
  But where's the fellow now?

MONK   No longer here,
  But banished far away.

LEPORELLO   Thank God for that.
  Let's hope it's far indeed. I'd have these rakes   85
  All bound in chains and thrown into the sea.

DON JUAN
  What drivel's this?

LEPORELLO   Be quiet, I'm attempting...

DON JUAN

  So this is where they buried the Commander?

MONK

  Indeed: his wife put up a monument
  And comes here every evening without fail   90
  To pray to God for his departed soul
  And weep.

DON JUAN   A strange, uncommon widow this!
  And pretty too?

MONK   We anchorites forbid
  A woman's beauty to affect our souls;
  But falsehood is a sin, and I admit: 95
  A saint himself could see her wondrous charms.

DON JUAN

  Then he who was her husband had good cause
  To be so jealous that he kept her hid,
  For none of us did ever see her face.
  I'd like to see her now and have a chat.   100

MONK

  Oh, Dona Anna never speaks with men.

DON JUAN

  And does she, holy father, speak with you?

MONK

  That's quite a different matter; I'm a monk.
  But here she comes.

                    (DONA ANNA enters.)

DONA ANNA   Unlock the gates, good father.

MONK

  At once; I've been expecting you, Senora.   105

                    (DONA ANNA follows the monk.)

LEPORELLO

  So, how's she look?

DON JUAN   I didn't see a thing
  Beneath those sombre widow's weeds—just glimpsed
  A bit of slender ankle as she passed.

LEPORELLO
  Oh, that'll do. Your keen imagination
  Will picture you the rest, I have no doubt;   110
  It's defter than a painter's brush, I swear.
  And never has it mattered where you start—
  With forehead or with foot, it's all the same.

DON JUAN
  O Leporello, you can be assured,
  I'll know the lady soon.

LEPORELLO (*to himself*)   Oh, not again!   115
  That's all we need! The husband he dispatched
  And now would see the grieving widow's tears.
  The shameless wretch!

DON JUAN   But look, the darkness falls.
  And so, before the moon ascends her throne
  And turns this inky black to glowing night,   120
  We'll see Madrid.

(*He leaves.*)

LEPORELLO   The Spanish grandee, thief-like,
  Awaits the night, yet fears the moon. O God!
  This cursèd life. How long must I endure
  This madman's ways? I lack the strength, I swear.

SCENE II

A room. Supper at Laura's

FIRST GUEST
  I tell you, Laura, never in your life
  Have you with such perfection played a role.
  You grasped the very essence of the part.

SECOND GUEST
  You played it to the hilt! With such emotion!

THIRD GUEST
  Such artistry you showed!

LAURA   Ah yes, tonight   5
  My every gesture, every word... was perfect.
  I totally succumbed to inspiration;
  The words poured forth—not lines I'd drily learned,
  But from my very soul itself...

FIRST GUEST   How true.
  And even now your eyes retain their glow,   10
  Your cheeks their flame; the passion in your heart
  Has not yet passed. Don't let it die, my dear,
  Or fruitless waste away; come, Laura, sing,
  We beg you, sing.

LAURA   Then hand me my guitar.

                    (*She sings.*)

ALL
  O brava, brava! Marvellous! Divine!   15

FIRST GUEST
  We thank you, sorceress; you charm our hearts.
  Of all the happy pleasures life supplies,
  To love alone does music yield in sweetness;

But love itself is melody... You see,
Your sullen guest, Don Carlos, too, is moved.   20

SECOND GUEST
What sounds! What depth of feeling in the words!
Who wrote them, Laura dear?

LAURA   Don Juan himself.

DON CARLOS
What's that? Don Juan!

LAURA   He wrote them long ago,
My ever faithful friend, my fickle love.

DON CARLOS
Your friend's a godless scoundrel and a wretch,   25
And you're a fool!

LAURA   Have you gone raving mad?
Take care: though Spanish grandee you may be,
I'll have my servants in to slit your throat.

DON CARLOS
Then call them now.

FIRST GUEST   Oh, Laura, stop it, please!
Don Carlos, hold your rage; she doesn't know...   30

LAURA
Know what? That in a duel, and honourably,
Don Juan his brother killed? He should have slain
Don Carlos here.

DON CARLOS   I've been a fool to rage.

LAURA
Since you yourself admit you've been a fool,
We'll make our peace.

DON CARLOS   Forgive me, Laura, please.   35
The fault was mine. But try to understand:
I cannot hear that name with mute indifference...

LAURA

    And yet am I to blame that every moment
    I find that very name upon my lips?

GUEST

    Come, Laura, show us that your anger's gone.   40
    Another song.

LAURA   All right, a parting song.
    It's late, and you must leave. Now let me see?...
    I have the song.

                  (*She sings.*)

ALL   Incomparable! What charm!

LAURA

    Now, gentlemen, good night.

GUESTS   Good night, dear Laura.

      (*They leave.* LAURA *detains* DON CARLOS.)

LAURA

    You madman, you! You'll stay with me tonight.   45
    I've taken quite a fancy to your looks;
    The way you ground your teeth when you maligned me
    Brought to my mind Don Juan.

DON CARLOS   That lucky man!
    You loved him then?

             (LAURA *nods.*)

          And very much?

LAURA   Oh, yes.

DON CARLOS

    And love him even now?

LAURA   This very moment?   50
    Oh, no... I never love two men at once;
    Just now... it's you I love.

DON CARLOS   But tell me, Laura,
    How old you are.

LAURA   I turned eighteen this year.

DON CARLOS
    You're young tonight... and young shall you remain
    For five or six more years. For six more years   55
    Will men, enamoured, crowd the path you walk,
    Caress and cherish you, and make you gifts,
    Amuse you with their nightly serenades,
    And strike each other down in murky alleys
    To win your love. But when your time has passed,   60
    When eyes have dimmed and wrinkled lids are dark,
    When strands of grey have streaked your lovely hair,
    And men have called you old and turned away,
    What then will you reply?

LAURA   Why ask me that?
    Why think about such things? What talk is this?   65
    Or do you always have such morbid thoughts?
    Come here... let's step outside. How soft the sky;
    How warm and still the evening air... the night
    Of laurel and of lemon smells; the moon...
    All gleaming in the deep and darkling blue...   70
    The watchman calling out his long: *All's well!*...
    While far away—in Paris to the north—
    The sky, perhaps, is overcast with clouds,
    A cold wind blows, and chilling rain descends;
    But what is that to us? Oh, Carlos, come...   75
    I order you to smile. That's better now!

DON CARLOS
    You charming devil!

                    (*A knock at the door.*)

DON JUAN   Laura, open up!

LAURA
    Whose voice is that? Who's there?

DON JUAN   Unlock the door...

LAURA
  It couldn't be!... O God!...

              (*She opens the door.* DON JUAN *enters.*)

DON JUAN   Hello.

LAURA   Don Juan!...

              (*She throws her arms around his neck.*)

DON CARLOS
  What's this! Don Juan!

DON JUAN   My sweet, my lovely girl!   80

                (*He kisses her.*)

  Who's with you there? Who is this man?

DON CARLOS   It's I,
  Don Carlos here.

DON JUAN   An unexpected meeting!
  Come morning, sir, I'm at your service.

DON CARLOS   No!
  This very moment... now!

LAURA   Don Carlos, stop!
  You're not upon the street—but in my house—   85
  Please leave at once.

DON CARLOS (*not listening*)
                  I'm still at your disposal,
  I do believe, you have your sword.

DON JUAN   Well then,
  Impatient friend, lay on!

                (*They fight.*)

LAURA   O God! Don Juan!...

        (*She throws herself on the bed.* DON CARLOS *falls.*)

DON JUAN
  Get up, my dear, it's finished now.

LAURA   Well then?
  He's dead? How marvellous! And in my room!   90
  And what am I to do, you devil's rake?
  And how shall I be rid of him?

DON JUAN   Perhaps,
  He's still alive?

LAURA (*examining the body*)
                Oh yes! Just look, you fiend,
  You didn't miss... you pierced him through the heart,
  There's not a drop of blood, nor does he breathe...   95
  What now, I say?

DON JUAN   There's nothing to be done,
  He called it on himself.

LAURA   O God, Don Juan,
  You vex me so. These constant escapades,
  Whose fault is never yours!... But where've you been?
  And when did you return?

DON JUAN   I've just arrived—   100
  And secretly at that; I've not been pardoned.

LAURA
  And right away you thought about your Laura?
  How sweet that you remembered. But alas,
  I don't believe a word. You happened by
  And chanced to see the house.

DON JUAN   Sweet Laura, no,   105
  Ask Leporello then. I've taken rooms
  Not far from town—some wretched inn—and came
  Into Madrid for you alone.

                    (*He kisses her.*)

LAURA   My sweet!...
  Oh, stop... Before the dead! But what of him?

DON JUAN
  Just let him lie: before the break of day   110
  I'll wrap him in my cloak and cart him off
  And drop him at a crossroad.

LAURA   But take care,
  Be sure that no one sees you in the light.
  What luck you didn't come a moment sooner!
  Your friends were here for supper, and, in fact,   115
  Had barely even left when you appeared.
  Imagine if you'd come while they were here!

DON JUAN
  But tell me, Laura, had you loved him long?

LAURA
  Loved whom? You must be mad.

DON JUAN   Oh come, confess:
  How often, since I left, have you been faithless?   120
  How many have you loved?

LAURA   And you, you rogue?

DON JUAN
  Confess... Ah no, we'll tell each other after.

SCENE III

The Commander's statue

DON JUAN
    All augurs well: since having slain Don Carlos,
    I've taken refuge here and have assumed
    The guise of simple monk. Each day I see
    My charming widow, who begins—I think—
    To notice me as well. We still remain   5
    On strictly formal terms, but I intend
    To speak with her today. The time has come!
    Yet how shall I begin? 'I dare intrude'...?
    Perhaps: 'Senora'...? Bah! I'll have no plan,
    I'll say whatever comes into my mind,   10
    I'll improvise my tender song of love...
    She'll be here soon. Without her, to be sure,
    The good Commander here seems rather bored.
    But what a huge colossus they've erected!
    Whereas in life he seemed quite small and feeble.   15
    Why, standing on his toes, that puny man
    Could not have touched his monstrous statue's nose.
    That day we met behind the Escurial,
    He fell upon my sword and stood transfixed,
    A dragonfly upon a pin—and yet,   20
    The man was proud and brave, and had some spirit.
    But here she comes.

(DONA ANNA *enters.*)

DONA ANNA   Again he's here... Good father,
    I fear that I disturb your meditations—
    Forgive me, please.

DON JUAN   Oh no, it's I, Senora,
    Should beg forgiveness here of you. Perchance,   25
    I hinder you from pouring out your grief.

DONA ANNA

No, father, all my grief lies deep within;
And here with you, the better may my prayers
To heaven rise. Indeed I'd be most grateful
To have you, father, join your voice with mine. 30

DON JUAN

To me... to me you offer such a boon!
O Dona Anna, I'm unfit for this.
These sinful lips of mine would never dare
To join with yours in holy supplication.
I dare but gaze—with reverence from afar— 35
When, bowing in a silent show of grief,
You drape with raven locks the pallid stone,
And it appears that I have just beheld
An angel come in secret to this tomb;
And then I find within this troubled heart 40
No hint of prayer—but only speechless wonder:
How happy he, I think, whose frigid grave
Is warmed by such an angel's airy sighs
And watered by her sweet and loving tears.

DONA ANNA

How strange I find these words you speak!

DON JUAN   Senora? 45

DONA ANNA

I haven't... you forget...

DON JUAN   That I am nought
But simple monk? That my unworthy voice
Ought never to be heard in such a place?

DONA ANNA

It seemed to me... Have I misunderstood?

DON JUAN

So then you've guessed; you know the truth, I see! 50

DONA ANNA

What truth is this?

DON JUAN   That I am not a monk.
I beg you on my knees for your forgiveness.

DONA ANNA
O God! Get up, get up... Who are you then?

DON JUAN
A wretch, the victim of my hopeless passion.

DONA ANNA
My God! To speak such things before this tomb!   55
Pray, leave at once.

DON JUAN   One minute, Dona Anna,
I beg of you!

DONA ANNA   But what if someone came!...

DON JUAN
The gates are locked. One minute, please! I beg!

DONA ANNA
What then? What is it that you want?

DON JUAN   To die.
Oh, let me die this moment at your feet,   60
And let my wretched dust be buried here;
Oh, not beside these ashes that you love,
But somewhere farther off—before the gate,
Inside the very entrance to this place,
That you might there caress my sorry grave   65
With touch of gentle foot or flowing cloak,
When coming here to grace this noble tomb
With lowered head and softly falling tears.

DONA ANNA
You must be mad.

DON JUAN   O lady, do you think
Such craving for the end a sign of madness?   70
If I were truly mad, 'twould be my wish
To stay alive, for then I'd have the hope

Of touching with my tender love your heart;
If I were truly mad, why then I'd come
To stand beneath your balcony at night 75
And haunt your very sleep with serenades;
No longer would I try to hide or flee,
But rather would I seek to catch your eye;
If I were truly mad, I'd not endure
In silence so much pain...

DONA ANNA   And this you think 80
Is silence, sir?

DON JUAN   'Twas chance, dear lady, chance
That made me speak—or else you'd ne'er have known
The secret sorrow deep within my heart.

DONA ANNA
And have you loved me so for very long?

DON JUAN
I know not, lady, whether long or not; 85
I only know that since that time alone
Have I perceived the preciousness of life
Or understood what happiness might mean.

DONA ANNA
Withdraw, I pray... I find you dangerous.

DON JUAN
How so... how so?

DONA ANNA   I'm frightened by your words. 90

DON JUAN
I'll hold my tongue, but do not drive away
A man whose only joy is in your face.
I entertain no hopes or fond illusions,
No claims do I advance but one alone:
That I may see your face if I be doomed 95
To stay upon this earth.

DONA ANNA   Withdraw... such words,
  Such ravings are unfit for where we are.
  Tomorrow you may call. And if you swear
  To hold me as before in full respect,
  I'll see you then—at evening, after dark;   100
  I have not entertained or seen a soul
  Since I've been widowed...

DON JUAN   Angel Dona Anna!
  May God console your heart, as you today
  Have eased the heart of one who greatly suffers.

DONA ANNA
  Now go, I say.

DON JUAN   One moment more, I pray.   105

DONA ANNA
  Then I must leave... for as it is my mind
  Is now untuned to prayer. Your worldly words
  Distract me from my vows. I've grown unused
  To hear such talk. Tomorrow, though... tomorrow—
  I'll see you then.

DON JUAN   I scarcely dare believe...   110
  I hardly dare surrender to my joy...
  Until tomorrow then! Not here, not here!
  And not by stealth!

DONA ANNA   Tomorrow, yes tomorrow.
  And your true name?

DON JUAN   Diego de Calvado.

DONA ANNA
  Farewell then, Don Diego.

(She leaves.)

DON JUAN   Leporello!   115

(LEPORELLO *enters.*)

LEPORELLO
Your pleasure, sir?

DON JUAN   My dearest Leporello!
I'm happy, man! 'At evening... after dark...'
Make ready, Leporello, for tomorrow...
I'm happy as a child!

LEPORELLO   You spoke with her?
And she, perhaps, responded to you kindly?   120
Or did you, master, give her then your blessing?

DON JUAN
No, Leporello, no! An assignation,
An assignation, do you hear!

LEPORELLO   Ye Gods!
Oh widows, are you all the same?

DON JUAN   I'm happy!
I want to sing, to hug the great wide world!   125

LEPORELLO
And what might the Commander have to say?

DON JUAN
You think, my friend, that he'll be jealous now?
I have my doubts; the man was always sane,
And surely since he died, he must have cooled.

LEPORELLO
But cast your eye upon his statue there.   130

DON JUAN
Why so?

LEPORELLO
          It looks on you, or so it seems,
In anger.

DON JUAN
          Go, good Leporello, then,

And say that I invite it to my house,
Or rather Dona Anna's on the morrow.

LEPORELLO
Invite the statue! Why?

DON JUAN   Oh, Leporello,   135
It's not for conversation, to be sure,—
But bid the statue come to Dona Anna's
At evening after dark... and there to stand
The watch beside her door.

LEPORELLO   Be careful, sir,
With whom you jest!

DON JUAN   Go to!

LEPORELLO   But sir...

DON JUAN   Go to.   140

LEPORELLO
O statue most illustrious and great!
My master here, Don Juan, most humbly begs
That you tomorrow come... O Lord, I can't,
I'm too afraid.

DON JUAN   You cur! You'll pay!

LEPORELLO   All right...
My master here, Don Juan, has bid you come   145
Tomorrow after dark... to take the watch...
Outside your lady's door...

                (*The* STATUE *nods assent.*)

                    Ah! Ah!

DON JUAN   What's there?

LEPORELLO
O God! I'll die!

DON JUAN   What's wrong?

LEPORELLO (*nodding his head*)   The statue! Ah!...

DON JUAN
  You bow!

LEPORELLO
        Not I, but it!

DON JUAN   What nonsense this?

LEPORELLO
  Go look you for yourself.

DON JUAN   Take care, you knave.   150

          (*He turns to the* STATUE.)

Commander, I invite you to your widow's,
Tomorrow after dark... where I shall be...
To stand the watch. What say you, will you come?

          (*The* STATUE *nods again.*)

  Almighty God!

LEPORELLO   I told you so...

DON JUAN   Let's go.

SCENE IV

Dona Anna's room

DON JUAN *and* DONA ANNA

DONA ANNA
Be welcome, Don Diego; but I fear,
My mournful conversation may well prove
Too trying for a guest: a widowed wife,
I constantly lament my grievous loss...
And weep, like April, even as I smile.   5
But why so mute?

DON JUAN   I feel a wordless joy
In being here alone with you at last,
My lovely Dona Anna... in your house!
And not before that lucky dead man's tomb,
No longer seeing you upon your knees   10
Before your marble spouse.

DONA ANNA   Oh, Don Diego,
Are you so jealous that my buried husband
Can cause you pain?

DON JUAN   I cannot have such thoughts,
Your husband was the man you chose.

DONA ANNA   Oh no,
My mother gave my hand to Don Alvaro,   15
For we were poor, and Don Alvaro rich.

DON JUAN
The lucky man! He brought but worthless wealth
To lay before an angel—and for this
He tasted all the joys of paradise!
If I had known you then, with what elation   20
My rank and all my riches I'd have paid,
Yes, all... for just one gracious glance from you.

I would have been your slave and held you sacred;
Your every wish I would have learned to guess,
To grant them ere they came, to make your life   25
One constant, magic realm of all desires.
But Fate, alas, had something else in store.

DONA ANNA

Oh, Don Diego, say no more: I sin
To heed your words. I cannot love again,
A widow must be true beyond the grave.   30
If only you could know how Don Alvaro
Adored me once! And he himself, I'm sure,
Would never have received a woman's love,
Had he been so bereft. He would have kept
His marriage vows for life.

DON JUAN   O Dona Anna,   35
Torment my heart no more with recollections
Of him you wed. You've punished me enough,
Although, perhaps, I've earned it well.

DONA ANNA   How so?
You are not tied, I think, by holy bonds
To someone else—and in your loving thus,   40
You do no wrong to heaven or to me.

DON JUAN
To you! O God!

DONA ANNA   You surely don't feel guilt
On my account? Or tell me why?

DON JUAN   Of this
I cannot speak.

DONA ANNA   What is this, Don Diego?
You've done me wrong? How so? I beg you, answer.   45

DON JUAN
I will not speak!

DONA ANNA   Diego, this is strange:
  I ask... demand... that you reply.

DON JUAN   No! Never!

DONA ANNA
  So this is how you serve my every wish?
  And what did you just now so boldly claim?
  That you'd give all to be my willing slave.   50
  You anger me, Diego; now reply:
  Of what are you to blame?

DON JUAN   I dare not speak,
  You'll look at me with hatred and revulsion.

DONA ANNA
  No, no. I pardon you before you speak,
  But I must know.

DON JUAN   You should not wish to know   55
  The terrible and deadly thing I've done.

DONA ANNA
  The deadly thing! You torture me, Diego;
  I have to know... What is it you conceal?
  And how can you have given me offence?
  I knew you not... I have no enemies,   60
  Nor none I had. The man who slew my spouse,
  But only he.

DON JUAN (*to himself*)
          The denouement approaches!

         (*to* DONA ANNA)

  You never knew the hapless wretch Don Juan,
  Is that not so?

DONA ANNA   In all my living days
  I never saw him, no.

DON JUAN   And does your heart   65
  Nurse hatred of the man?

DONA ANNA   So honour bids.
But you're attempting to evade my question;
Now answer me, Diego, if you please...
I must insist.

DON JUAN   And what if you should chance
To meet Don Juan?

DONA ANNA   Why then, I'd thrust a dagger   70
Into the villain's heart.

DON JUAN   O Dona Anna!
Then thrust your dagger here!

DONA ANNA   Good Lord, Diego!
What's this?

DON JUAN   I'm not Diego... I'm Don Juan.

DONA ANNA
O God! It can't be so, I don't believe it.

DON JUAN
Don Juan am I.

DONA ANNA   It can't be true.

DON JUAN   It's true,   75
I killed your husband—and regret it not;
And there is no repentance in my soul.

DONA ANNA
What's this I hear? Oh no! It cannot be.

DON JUAN
Don Juan am I, and I'm in love with you.

DONA ANNA (*fainting*)
Where am I! Where? I'm faint... I'm faint...

DON JUAN   Good Lord!   80
What's wrong with her? What is it, Dona Anna?
Wake up, wake up, come rouse yourself; Diego,
Your loving slave, is at your feet.

DONA ANNA   Oh, leave!

(weakly)

My greatest foe... you took away my life...
My life... my very life...

DON JUAN   Sweet creature, speak!   85
And I'll requite you for the blow I struck,
Pronounce my sentence as I kneel before you:
At your command... I die; or bid me breathe
For you alone.

DONA ANNA   Is this the real Don Juan...

DON JUAN
No doubt, you've often heard the man described   90
As villain or as fiend. O Dona Anna...
Such ill repute may well in part be true:
My weary conscience bears a heavy load
Of evil deeds. For all too many years
I've been the most devoted slave of lust;   95
But ever since the day I saw your face,
I feel reborn, restored once more to life;
In loving you, I've learned to love true goodness,
And now for once I bend my trembling knees
And kneel in awe before almighty virtue.   100

DONA ANNA
Ah, yes, Don Juan is eloquent, I know;
I've heard of his seductive way with words,
They say that you're a godless and depraved,
Inhuman fiend. How many hapless women
Have you destroyed?

DON JUAN   But not a one till now   105
Have I in truth adored.

DONA ANNA   Should I believe
That now at last Don Juan has come to love,
And not to seek another of his victims?

DON JUAN

Had I intended, lady, to deceive you,
Would I have made confession or revealed   110
The very name you cannot bear to hear?
What kind of plot or craftiness is this?

DONA ANNA

Who knows your heart? Why visit me at all?
You might have been detected on the way,
And then you would have met... not me, but death.   115

DON JUAN

I fear not death. For one sweet moment here
I'd give my life without complaint.

DONA ANNA   But how,
You reckless man, will you escape from here?

DON JUAN (*kissing her hand*)

So even you can find within your heart
Some pity for Don Juan! O Dona Anna,   120
Have you no hatred in your angel's soul?

DONA ANNA

I wish with all my heart that I could hate you!
But I'm afraid... that you and I must part.

DON JUAN

And when shall we two meet again?

DONA ANNA   Who knows.
One day, perhaps.

DON JUAN

                    Tomorrow?

DONA ANNA   Where?

DON JUAN   Right here.   125

DONA ANNA

Alas, Don Juan, how weak my woman's heart.

DON JUAN

In pledge of your forgiveness... one brief kiss...

DONA ANNA

It's late... it's late.

DON JUAN   One cold, one quiet kiss...

DONA ANNA

As you will have it so... one kiss I grant...

(*A knock at the door.*)

What noise was that?... Conceal yourself, Don Juan!   130

DON JUAN

Farewell... until we meet, my tender friend.

(*He leaves, then rushes in again.*)

Ah, no!

DONA ANNA

    What is it? Ah!...

(*The* STATUE *of the Commander enters.*)
(DONA ANNA *faints.*)

STATUE   You summoned me.

DON JUAN

O God! O Dona Anna!

STATUE   Let her be.

It's finished. Do you tremble now, Don Juan?

DON JUAN

Oh, no. I called you here... and bid you welcome.   135

STATUE

Then come... your hand.

DON JUAN

    Ah, yes... my hand. O God!

How cold and hard his mighty fist of stone!

Away from me... let go... let go my hand...
I perish... all is finished... Dona Anna!...

>(*They sink into the ground.*)

IV

A FEAST IN TIME OF PLAGUE

An excerpt from Wilson's tragedy,
The City of the Plague

A street. A table laid for a feast

Several men and women Celebrants

YOUNG MAN

   Most honoured Chairman! I would speak
   Of one whose memory we revere,
   A man whose jests and comic tales,
   Whose pointed wit and observations,
   So caustic with their mocking air,   5
   Enlivened many past occasions
   And drove away the gloom with which
   Our guest, the Plague, has now infected
   So many of our brightest minds.
   But two days since we hailed with mirth   10
   Those tales of his, and so tonight,
   Amid our feast, let's not forget
   Our Jackson now. Here stands his chair,
   The empty seat as if awaiting
   That merry man—but now he's gone   15
   To lie beneath the chilly earth...
   Although his vivid voice remains,
   Unsilenced yet within the grave;
   But we are many still alive
   And have tonight no cause to grieve.   20
   So I propose for Jackson's sake
   A ringing toast and shouts of cheer,
   As if he lived.

MASTER OF REVELS

            He was the first
   To leave our band. And so let's drink
   A silent toast.

YOUNG MAN   So be it then.   25

                (All drink in silence.)

MASTER OF REVELS

    Your voice, dear Mary, can evoke
    The dark rich sounds of native song;
    So sing us, Mary, something sad,
    That we may then more madly still
    To mirth return, like one who wakes   30
    From some dark dream to earth again.

MARY (*sings*)

                Long ago our land was blessed:
                Peaceful, rich, and gay;
                People then on days of rest
                Filled the church to pray;   35
                Children's voices full of cheer
                Through the schoolyard rang,
                In the fields both far and near
                Scythe and sickle sang.

                Now the church deserted stands;   40
                School is locked and dark;
                Overgrown are all our lands;
                Empty groves are stark;
                Now the village, bare as bone,
                Seems an empty shell—   45
                All is still—the graves alone
                Thrive and toll the bell.

                Endless carts of dead appear;
                Now the living cry,
                Calling down in mortal fear   50
                Mercy from on high.
                Endless corpses all demand
                Plots of hallowed ground,
                Graves like frightened cattle stand
                Crowded close all round.   55

                If my youth is doomed to go
                Early into night,—

Edmund, whom I treasure so,
Edmund, my delight,
Don't approach your Jenny's bier,   60
Please, I beg, be kind;
Do not kiss these lips once dear,
Follow far behind.

Leave the village then, I pray,
Find some place of peace,   65
Dull your pain and go away,
Bring your soul release.
When the plague has passed, my love,
Pay my dust its due;
Even, Edmund, up above,   70
Jenny will be true.

MASTER OF REVELS

We thank you, Mary, pensive lass,
We thank you for your mournful air.
In former days some plague like ours
Attacked your lovely hills and vales,   75
And woeful moans back then arose
Above your streams and purling brooks,
Which now once more in joy and peace
Meander through your native realm;
And now that dreadful year that took   80
So many brave and noble souls
Has only left the barest trace
In this your simple, rustic song,
So touching and so sad... There's nought
Could move us more at this our feast   85
Than sounds remembered by the heart.

MARY

If only I had never learned
To sing such songs so far from home!
My parents loved their Mary's voice,
And even now I seem to hear   90

Myself in song outside our door.
My voice was sweeter then and sang
In tones more pure and true.

LOUISA   Such songs
Are out of fashion now. And yet,
There still are simple souls who pine   95
At women's tears... and deem them real.
Our Mary thinks a tearful eye
Invincible,—but if she thought
Her laughter so, then be assured,
She'd laugh and laugh. But Walsingham   100
Has praised these shrieking northern belles,
And so she moans. Oh how I loathe
These Scottish heads of flaxen hair!

MASTER OF REVELS
Be still. I hear the wagon wheels.

(*A cart goes by, laden with corpses and
driven by a black man.*)

MASTER OF REVELS
Louisa swoons! To hear her talk,   105
You'd think her heart was like a man's.
The cruel prove weaker than the soft,
And dread can strike the fiercest soul.
Some water, Mary... she'll come round.

MARY
Come, sister of my shame and woe,   110
Lean back on me.

LOUISA (*regaining consciousness*)
                         I thought I saw
Some dreadful thing—all black... white-eyed.
That called me to its cart... and there
The dead lay deep... and babbled words...
Some strange and unfamiliar tongue...   115
But tell me, did I only dream?
Or did that cart go by?

YOUNG MAN   Louisa!
   Lift up your heart. Although our street
   Is refuge safe enough from death,
   A place for feasts, where grief is banned,   120
   That sombre cart, as you well know,
   Has right to travel where it will,
   And let it pass we must. But now,
   Good Walsingham, let's cancel strife
   And all these women's fainting spells.   125
   Come, sing a rash and lively song,
   No tune composed of Scottish grief—
   But reckless, bacchanalian song,
   One fit for friends and flaming cups!

MASTER OF REVELS
   I know no songs like this. I'll sing   130
   A hymn to plagues. I wrote the thing
   Last night when we had quit the feast.
   A strange, compulsive need for rhyme,
   Quite new to me, then gripped my soul.
   My throaty voice well suits the song...   135

VOICES FROM THE CROWD
   A hymn to plagues! Let's hear it then!
   A hymn to plagues! Bravó! Well done!

MASTER OF REVELS (*sings*)
      When mighty Winter from the north,
      Like warrior chieftain, marches forth
      To lead herself her ragged host   140
      Of frosts and snows against the land,
      Our glasses ring in hearty toast
      And crackling chimneys warm our band.

      The Plague herself, that fearsome Queen,
      Has now arrived upon the scene   145
      To reap corruption's rich reward;
      All day and night with dreadful spade

She taps the battened windowboard.
But where to turn? Where summon aid?

As we from prankster Winter hide,   150
We'll greet the Plague locked up inside;
We'll light the flame and pour the wine,
We'll drown our thoughts and gaily jest,
And as we dance and as we dine,
We'll praise the reign of Empress Pest.   155

There's rapture on the battleground,
And where the black abyss is found,
And on the raging ocean main,
Amid the stormy waves of death,
And in the desert hurricane,   160
And in the Plague's pernicious breath.

For all that threatens to destroy
Conceals a strange and savage joy—
Perhaps for mortal man a glow
That promises eternal life;   165
And happy he who comes to know
This rapture found in storm and strife.

So hail to you, repellent Pest!
You strike no fear within our breast;
We are not crushed by your design;   170
So fill the foaming glasses high,
We'll sip the rosy maiden wine
And kiss the lips where plague may lie!

(*An aged* PRIEST *appears.*)

PRIEST
    This godless feast! You godless men!
    With revels and with wanton songs   175
    You mock the dark and gruesome hush
    Sent forth by death across the land!

At dreadful funeral rites I pray
Before the pale and weeping crowd,
While your repulsive sinful play   180
Disturbs the graveyard's silent peace
And shakes the earth where dead men sleep.
Had not old men's and women's prayers
Redeemed our common pit of death,
I might have thought that fiends had come   185
To torture sinners' godless souls
And drag them, cackling, off to hell.

SEVERAL VOICES

He speaks of hell as one who knows.
Be gone, old man, you've lost your way.

PRIEST

I charge you by the sacred blood   190
Of Him who suffered for our sins
To halt this monstrous feast, if still
You hope to meet by Heaven's grace
The souls of those you loved and lost.
Disperse, I say, and get you home!   195

MASTER OF REVELS

Our homes are sad—youth treasures mirth.

PRIEST

Can that be you, good Walsingham?
Who on your knees but three weeks since
Embraced your mother's corpse and sobbed?
Who howled and beat upon her grave?   200
Or think you that she doesn't weep
Great bitter tears in heaven now,
To see her son at such a feast,
This feast of vice—to hear your voice
In shameless song—all this amid   205
Our holy prayers and anguished sighs?
Come with me now!

MASTER OF REVELS   Why do you come
   To cause me pain? I cannot leave
   To take your path: what holds me here
   Is foul despair and memories dread,   210
   Awareness of my lawless ways,
   The horror of the deathly hush
   That now prevails within my house,—
   And yes, these fresh and frenzied revels,
   The blessèd poison of this cup,   215
   And kisses sweet (forgive me, Lord)
   From this depraved, but lovely wretch...
   My mother's shade will call me back
   No more... too late... I hear your plea
   And know you struggle for my soul...   220
   Too late... Depart, old man, in peace;
   But curst be all who follow thee.

SEVERAL VOICES
   Bravó! Well said! Our worthy chief!
   You've heard the sermon. Leave us, priest!

PRIEST
   Mathilda's blessèd spirit calls!   225

MASTER OF REVELS (*rising*)
   Oh, raise your pale, decrepit hand
   And swear to God to leave unspoke
   That name entombed forevermore!
   Oh, could I from those deathless eyes
   Conceal this scene! She thought me once   230
   A proud and pure... a noble man,
   And in my arms she savoured joy...
   Where am I now? My blessèd light!
   I see you... but my sinful soul
   Can reach you there no more...

A WOMAN'S VOICE   He's mad—   235
   He babbles of his buried wife.

PRIEST

Come with me now...

MASTER OF REVELS   In Heaven's name,
Good father, leave.

PRIEST   God save your soul.
Farewell, my son.

(He leaves. The feast goes on.)
(The MASTER OF REVELS *remains, lost in thought.)*

RUSALKA
(THE WATER-NYMPH)

The bank of the Dnieper, a mill

The MILLER *and his* DAUGHTER

MILLER
I swear, you stupid girls, you're all the same—
No brains at all. When some good man turns up,
A proper catch, and not some common sort,
You need to wrap him up and not let go.
And how? Through commonsense and right behaviour,   5
Enticing and rebuffing him by turns;
And now and then, in passing as it were,
To hint at marriage,—but above all look
To keep your precious maidenhead intact—
That priceless gift—it's like a spoken word—   10
Once let it go, you'll never get it back.
Or if, for marriage, there's no hope at all,
You ought at least to profit in some way,
Or benefit your kin; you have to think:
'He won't forever love me like today   15
And pamper me with gifts.' But no, not you!
You'd never think of reaping while you can!
Whenever he appears, you turn to mush;
You cater to his every whim and wish;
You hang about his neck the whole day long,—   20
Then all at once... your charming fellow's gone,
He's disappeared without a trace. And you?
You're left with nothing. Oh, you stupid girls!
I've told you this a hundred times or more:
Look out, my girl, and don't be such a fool,   25
To throw away good fortune when it comes;
Don't let the Prince escape, or waste yourself
By giving in too soon. And all for what?
So you can weep forever and lament
What's lost and gone.

DAUGHTER   But why are you so sure,   30
  He won't be back? That he's abandoned me?

MILLER
  Well, so it seems! How many times a week,
  At first, did he come hanging round the mill?
  Each blessèd day he came and, oftentimes,
  Came twice a day... but now he's slackened off   35
  And hardly comes—we haven't seen him now
  For nine whole days. And why is that, my girl?

DAUGHTER
  He must be busy; he has lots to do.
  He's not some miller, with a water-wheel
  To do his work. I've often heard him say,   40
  That no one bears such burdens as a prince.

MILLER
  Oh, come! You want to know what princes do?
  They send their hounds to ravage fox and hare,
  Insult the neighbours at their lavish feasts,
  And take in simple girls the like of you.   45
  Oh, yes, he works so hard, the poor, poor man!
  While I just sit, and let the water run!...
  Why, I've no moment's peace by day or night;
  There's always something to repair—some leak,
  Some rotting board! If you'd have had the sense   50
  To ask the Prince for just a bit of cash
  To mend the mill, we'd both be better off.

DAUGHTER
  My heart!

MILLER   What's wrong?

DAUGHTER   I hear the sound of hooves!
  His horse... It's he, it's he!

MILLER   Now look you, girl,
  Remember my advice, and don't forget...   55

DAUGHTER
    He's here, he's come!

    (*The* PRINCE *enters. His* EQUERRY *leads off his horse.*)

PRINCE   My greetings, dearest friend,
    And you, too, Miller.

MILLER   My most gracious Prince,
    You're welcome here indeed. It's been so long
    Since last we looked upon your shining eyes.
    I'll go at once to make you some refreshment.   60

                    (*He leaves.*)

DAUGHTER
    You've finally remembered me, my love!
    You ought to be ashamed to let me suffer,
    To torture me with such an endless wait.
    What terrible imaginings I've known!
    What dreadful dreams have shrivelled up my soul!   65
    I thought your horse might suddenly have bolted,
    And thrown you in a swamp or down a cliff;
    That bears had overcome you in the woods,
    That you were ill... or out of love with me...
    But thank the Lord, you're still alive and whole,   70
    And love me as you always have, my Prince.
    Oh, say it's so.

PRINCE   As much as ever, angel.
    No, even more.

HIS LOVER   And yet, you look so sad.
    What troubles you, my love?

PRINCE   Do I seem sad?
    You just imagine it... I'm full of joy,   75
    As always, when I see your face.

SHE   Not so,
    When full of joy, you hasten to my side,
    I hear your voice call out: 'Where are you, dove,

How fares my lass?' And then you kiss my lips,
And ask me if I'm happy that you're here,   80
And whether I expected you so soon.
But now—you hear my words and barely speak,
Don't hold me close, or even kiss my eyes.
There's something wrong, I know. What is it, love?
I haven't somehow angered you, I hope?   85

PRINCE

I'd rather shun dissembling and pretence.
You're right, alas; my heart is full of woe—
A heavy grief that even you, my love,
With all your sweet caresses, cannot lift,
Or help assuage, or even share with me.   90

SHE

But tell me what it is, this secret woe;
It's agony to see you grieve alone.
Allow me, and I'll share your grief; if not,
I won't annoy you with a single tear.

PRINCE

Why drag it out? The sooner done, the better.   95
My tender friend, you know as well as I,
There is no lasting happiness on earth:
Not rank or beauty, neither wealth nor power—
Can shield us from the heavy blows of fate.
And we've been happy—haven't we, my dove?—   100
The two of us; I know that I at least
Have found great joy in you and in your love.
And so, whatever fate may hold in store,
Wherever I may go, I'll think of you.
In losing you, my dear, I know I've lost   105
A treasure that can never be replaced.

SHE

I still don't understand you, or your words,
And yet I fear... some dreadful, dark undoing,

Some unforeseen misfortune fate prepares.
Not separation, though?

PRINCE   You've guessed the truth.   110
Our separation has been willed by fate.

SHE
But what could part us? If you have to leave—
Wherever you might go, I'd follow gladly;
I'll dress up as a boy and be your valet...
I'll serve you, if you let me, on the march,   115
In war itself—I'm not afraid of war—
If only I can see you and be near...
It isn't true. You're only testing me,
Or teasing me, my love, with idle jests.

PRINCE
I'm in no jesting mood today, I fear,   120
Nor do I need to put you to the test.
It's not a journey to a distant land,
Or call to war—I'm staying here at home,
But still... this separation must be final.

SHE
I see. I think I understand it now...   125
You're marrying.

                    (*The* PRINCE *is silent.*)

                    You're marrying!

PRINCE   I must.
So try to understand. Unlike young girls,
A prince is never free to heed his heart;
His choice is made by others for their needs.
Both God and time will bring you consolation.   130
Remember me, and as a keepsake take
This headband—Come... I'll help you put it on.
And here, take this, this string of pearls I brought.
And one thing more: I made a promise once
To give your father this. Please pass it on.   135

(He hands her a bag of gold.)

Goodbye.

SHE   But wait. There's something else... I think...
I'm trying to remember...

PRINCE   Yes.

SHE   For you
I'd gladly give... that isn't it... Oh, wait!
I can't believe that you'd abandon me
Forever... No... that's still not right... What was it?   140
Yes! I remember now: today I felt
Your baby stirring underneath my heart.

PRINCE
Unhappy girl! There's nothing to be done.
You must be strong, for him at least. I swear,
I won't desert you, and I'll help the child.   145
In time, perhaps, I'll even come myself
To see you both. Take comfort now, don't cry.
I'll hold you in my arms one final time.

(as he leaves)

Thank God it's done—I feel a bit relieved.
I thought there'd be a scene, but all in all,   150
It went quite smoothly.

(He leaves. She remains motionless.)

MILLER *(entering)*   Would you care, my lord,
To join us in the mill?... Where is he, girl?
What's happened to the Prince? Aha, look here!
A handsome headband! And adorned with gems!
How bright it glows! And pearls as well!... Indeed,   155
A princely gift. He's been our benefactor!
And here, what's this? This bag! Not gold, perchance?
Why don't you answer me? What is it, girl?
You haven't said a word. Or are you numb?

In shock at such an unexpected joy?
Has lockjaw got your tongue?

DAUGHTER   I loved him so.
   I can't believe it's true... it can't be true.
   Is he a savage beast? Or is his heart
   So coarse and brutish?

MILLER   What's the matter, girl?

DAUGHTER
   Oh, tell me, father, what I could have done   165
   To vex him so? In just a week, one week,
   Is all my beauty gone?... Or has some witch
   Put poison in his drink?

MILLER   What's wrong with you?

DAUGHTER
   He's left me, father. And he's riding off!—
   And, like a mindless wretch, I let him go,   170
   I didn't try to clasp him by his mantle,
   Or hang upon the bridle of his horse!
   I should have let him vent his angry spleen
   By hacking off my arms above the wrist,
   Or trampling me beneath his horse's hooves.   175

MILLER
   You're mad!

DAUGHTER   You see, these princes, when they wed,
   Aren't free, like girls, to listen to their hearts;
   They're only free, it seems, to lead you on,
   Swear solemn oaths, entice you with their tears,
   And say: I'll fly you to the secret room,   180
   The gilded chamber of my castle keep;
   I'll clothe you in brocade and crimson velvet...
   They're free to teach poor girls to rise at night,
   And hasten at their whistles in the dark
   To meet behind the mill until the dawn.   185

Their princely hearts are entertained to hear
Our petty woes... and then it's just—goodbye,
Go wander where you will, my pretty thing,
Go love some other chap.

MILLER   So that's it then.

DAUGHTER
But who's his bride? I wonder whom he chose   190
To take my place? I'll find out who she is,
I'll deal with her—I'll tell the witch straight out:
Keep off the Prince,—two she-wolves never hunt
In one ravine.

MILLER   You're such a witless fool!
If now the Prince has picked himself a bride,   195
Who says he can't? That's just the way it is.
I've told you all along...

DAUGHTER   And he could act
So like a decent man, just take his leave,
And give me presents as a fine farewell!
And money, too!—and all to buy me off!   200
To stop my tongue by stuffing it with silver,
To spare his reputation any taint,
And keep it from his sweet young wife, no doubt.
Oh, yes... I can't forget... he also said
To pass along this silver for your help,   205
For raising such a loose and wanton girl,
And flaunting her about... You've made out well
By my disgrace.

(*She gives him the bag.*)

FATHER (*in tears*) It's come to this! Oh, God!
That ever I should hear such words! How cruel
To heap such foul abuse upon your father.   210
And you my only child in all this world,
The only comfort of my grim old age.
I couldn't help but pamper you a bit.

And look how God has punished me for this,
For my paternal weakness.

DAUGHTER   Aah, I'm choking!   215
An icy snake is pressing on my neck...
He's wrapped a snake about my throat, a snake!
A snake, not pearls!

>   (*She tears off the string of pearls.*)

MILLER   You're not yourself!

DAUGHTER   Just so
I'd tear you limb from limb, you snaky witch,
You cursèd thief that took my lover's heart!   220

MILLER
You're raving, daughter, raving.

DAUGHTER (*taking off the headband*)
                                    Take my crown,
My crown of shame! With this the cunning fiend
Did crown me as a bride, when I renounced
All precious things I used to treasure so.
We stand uncrowned. Away with you, my crown!   225

>   (*She throws the headband into the Dnieper.*)

All's finished now.

>   (*She throws herself into the river.*)

THE OLD MAN (*collapsing*)
                    The horror... Oh, the horror!

The Prince's Palace

A wedding. The BRIDE *and* GROOM *at table.*
Guests. A choir of young girls

MATCHMAKER

A happy rite we celebrate this day.
Good health, our youthful Princess and our Prince.
God grant you many years of love and joy!
And grant to us more feasting at your table.
But why, my beauties, are your voices mute?   5
Why, lovely swans, have you become so still?
Or have you now exhausted all your songs?
Or has your singing parched your tender throats?

CHOIR

Make a match, or make a match,
Silly fool, go make a match!   10
Off you went to fetch the bride,
In the garden turned aside,
Emptied out a keg of beer,
Poured it on the cabbage ear,
Down before the fence you bowed,   15
To the gate you prayed aloud:
Help me, gate-post, find the way,
Show me, if you will, good gate,
How to find the bridegroom's mate.
Guess how you can win the day,   20
See that bulging purse you wear,
Hear that money jingling there?
That's what lures the maidens fair.

MATCHMAKER

You naughty things, a sorry song you've picked!
But here, take this, and make no more complaint.   25

(*He gives the girls some money.*)

A LONE VOICE

Across the pebbles and the yellow sand
A little brook went splashing by,
And in that brook two fishes swam,
Two golden sunfish flashing by:
And have you heard, my sister dear,   30
The latest news our river's had?
Just yesterday a maiden drowned,
And, drowning, cursed her charming lad.

MATCHMAKER

My pretty ones! What sort of song is that?
It's not a song for weddings, not at all.   35
Who chose the thing? Speak up, you girls.

THE GIRLS   Not I.
Nor I... It wasn't us.

MATCHMAKER   Who sang it then?

       (Confusion and whispering among the girls.)

PRINCE

I think I know.

      (He leaves the table and whispers to his equerry.)

      She's somewhere hereabout.
Remove the girl at once. And find the fool
Who dared to let her in.

      (The EQUERRY *goes up to the girls.)*

PRINCE *(sitting down, to himself)*
      She must have come   40
To do some mischief, or to raise a fuss,
To cover me with such a sense of shame,
I'd hang my head.

EQUERRY   I couldn't find her, sir.

PRINCE

Go look again. I know she's here. It's she
Who sang that awful song.

A GUEST   What splendid mead!   45
  It staggers legs and makes the head go round—
  Too tart, alas: it calls for something sweet.

　　　　(*The* PRINCE *and his* BRIDE *kiss. A faint cry is heard.*)

PRINCE
  She's here! That jealous cry was hers.

　　　　　　(*He turns to the* EQUERRY.)

　　　　　　　　　　　　What now?

EQUERRY
  She's nowhere to be found, my lord.

PRINCE   You fool.

BEST MAN (*getting up*)
  It's time to sprinkle hops upon the pair,   50
  And let the restless husband claim his bride.

　　　　　　　(*All rise.*)

CO-MATCHMAKER (*a woman*)
  High time, indeed. Bring on the cockerel.

　　　　(*The bride and groom are served roasted cockerel,
　　　　　　then showered with hops and led to their door.*)

CO-MATCHMAKER
  Don't cry, my little Princess, don't be scared;
  Be dutiful.

　　　　(*The* BRIDE *and* GROOM *retire to their bedroom;
　　the* CO-MATCHMAKER *and* BEST MAN *stay; the others leave.*)

BEST MAN　A cup of wine! Tonight
  I'll ride beneath their window till the dawn.   55
  A bit of wine, I'd say, would suit me well.

CO-MATCHMAKER (*pouring him a cup*)
  Drink up in health, good fellow.

BEST MAN   Aah! My thanks.
　　It came off rather well, I think, don't you?
　　A proper feast indeed.

CO-MATCHMAKER   The Lord be praised,
　　It all went well... but one thing troubles me.   60

BEST MAN
　　What's that?

CO-MATCHMAKER
　　　　　　　That song they sang, it bodes no good;
　　God knows, it wasn't any wedding song!

BEST MAN
　　A wretched bunch, those girls... they can't resist
　　Their silly pranks. I've never seen the like—
　　To tamper with the wedding of a prince.   65
　　Well, time to saddle up and do my rounds.
　　Good night, good mother.

(*He leaves.*)

CO-MATCHMAKER   Evil days to come!
　　This marriage is ill-made and frights my soul.

A Palace chamber

The PRINCESS and her NURSE

PRINCESS

   The trumpets sound! And yet, he doesn't come.
   Oh, nanny dear, when we were still betrothed,
   He never left my side; those days, it seemed,
   He couldn't feast his eyes on me enough.
   But after we were married, all was changed.   5
   He wakes me now before the break of dawn
   And sends to have his horse and saddle brought;
   Then gallops off till dark—though God knows where;
   Once home, he scarcely speaks a tender word,
   Can hardly bear to touch me, so it seems,   10
   Or give my pallid face a soft caress.

NURSE

   A man is like a rooster, dearest heart:
   He's cock-a-doo, and flap-a-wing... and fly!
   A woman, though, is like a brooding hen:
   She keeps her nest and hatches out her chicks.   15
   While still a groom, a man just hangs about,
   Won't eat or drink, can't get his fill of you.
   But once he's wed—there's this and that to do:
   He's got to see the neighbours, don't you know,
   Or ride with all his falcons to the hunt,   20
   Or when the devil calls—go off to war.
   He's here and there; he's everywhere but home.

PRINCESS

   But tell me, nanny, do you think he has
   A secret love?

NURSE   Don't even think such thoughts:
   Why, how could he prefer some other lass?   25
   You've won him with your beauty and your mind,
   Your breeding and your gentleness. Just think:

Wherever could he find so fine a wife,
A treasure such as you?

PRINCESS

    If only God would listen to my prayers   30
    And send me children, nanny! Then for sure
    I'd win him back and have his love again...
    That noise! The hunters have returned! He's here!...
    Why don't I see my husband in the crowd?

                (*A* HUNTSMAN *enters.*)

    What's happened to the Prince?

HUNTSMAN   He sent us back.   35

PRINCESS
    And he himself?

HUNTSMAN   The Prince has stayed behind,
    Within the wood that flanks the Dnieper's shore.

PRINCESS
    You left him all alone and unattended!
    What loyal servants of the Prince you are!
    Return at once, and at the gallop go!   40
    And tell him it was I who sent you back.

             (*The* HUNTSMAN *leaves.*)

    Oh, God in heaven! In the woods at night,
    With savage beasts and desperate men abroad,
    Where evil spirits roam and danger lurks.
    Oh, nanny, quick, we'll light the icon lamp.   45

NURSE
    At once, dear heart, at once.

The Dnieper. Night

WATER-NYMPHS

A joyous assembly,
From waters below
We rise in the moonlight
To bask in its glow.

Late at night we sisters gladly   5
Quit the deep in which we lie,
Rising from the river madly,
Bursting forth to reach the sky;
We can hear each other crying,
Voices ringing through the air,   10
As we shake our long and drying
Strands of green and dripping hair.

FIRST WATER-NYMPH

Underneath the bushes – hush!
Something's hiding in the brush.

SECOND WATER-NYMPH

Here between the earth and moon   15
Someone's creeping through the gloom.

(*They disappear.*)

PRINCE

How well I know this melancholy place!
I recognize the landmarks all about...
There stands the mill! It's all in ruins now,
The cheerful sound of water-wheels gone mute,   20
The millstone, too; the miller's dead, I guess.
He didn't mourn his hapless daughter long...
And here's the path—all overgrown by now,
No soul has passed this way for many years;
Nearby there was a garden with a fence...   25
Can that be it—that dense and tangled thicket?

Ah, there's the hallowed oak, the spot where she,
Embracing me, fell mute and hung her head...
How strange...

(*He goes up to the tree, whose leaves are falling.*)

I wonder what it means? These leaves,
They withered all at once, curled up and died,   30
And drifted down like ashes on my head.
And there it stands, the oak... all black and bare,
Like some accursèd thing.

(*An* OLD MAN *enters, ragged and half-naked.*)

OLD MAN   Good day, my son.

PRINCE
And who are you?

OLD MAN   The raven of these parts.

PRINCE
Oh, God, the miller!

OLD MAN   No... I have no mill!   35
I sold it to the ghosts behind the stove,
And gave the money to a water-nymph,
My prophet-daughter, so she'd keep it safe.
It's buried in the Dnieper river sand;
A one-eyed fish stands watch and guards it close.   40

PRINCE
Unhappy creature, he's gone mad. His thoughts
Are scattered like the clouds a storm has whipped.

OLD MAN
Why didn't you drop in the other night?
We had a feast and waited for you, Prince.

PRINCE
Who waited for me?

OLD MAN　　　　　　　　Why, my girl, of course.　　　　　45
But I just look the other way, you know,
So suit yourself; she'll stay with you all night,
Till cockcrow, if you want. And don't you fear,
I'll never breathe a word.

PRINCE　　　　　　　　Unhappy miller!

OLD MAN
I'm not a miller! Are you hard-a-hearing?　　　　　50
A raven, not a miller. It was strange:
That day she flung herself (do you remember?)
Into the raging stream, I followed her,
To leap from that same rock—when, suddenly,
I felt two mighty wings begin to sprout,　　　　　55
They grew beneath my arms in just a trice,
And bore me to the sky! And ever since,
I fly about, and now and then I peck
At rotting cows, or perch upon a grave
And caw a bit.

PRINCE　　　　　How pitiful he is!　　　　　60
And who looks after you?

OLD MAN　　　　　　　　They care for me,
Oh, yes, they do. I'm very old, you know,
And full of mischief, too. But thank the Lord,
The little water-nymph is here.

PRINCE　　　　　　　　　Who's that?

OLD MAN
My daughter's girl.

PRINCE　　　　　I can't make head or tail　　　　　65
Of what he says. These woods are harsh, old man,
You'll starve to death out here, or else some beast
Will eat your flesh. You'd better leave these woods;
Come live with me.

OLD MAN　　　　That place of yours? No, thanks.
You'd lure me in, and once you had me there,　　　　　70

You'd strangle me with pearls. I'd rather stay
Where I'm alive and well. Your palace? No!

(*He leaves.*)

PRINCE
It's all my fault! How terrible it is
To lose one's wits. It's easier to die.
We treat a corpse, at least, with some respect,   75
And keep him in our prayers. For in the end,
Death makes us all the same. But when a man
Has lost his reason, he's a man no more.
What use the gift of speech for one whose mind
Has no control of words; his only kin   80
Are savage beasts; and people mock his ways
And toy with him, and God withdraws His grace.
The poor old man! The sight of him provokes
The torments of remorse within my soul!

HUNTSMAN
He's here! We thought we'd never find you, sir!   85

PRINCE
What brings you here?

HUNTSMAN   The princess sent us back.
She feared for you, my lord.

PRINCE   I can't abide
Her constant watchfulness! Am I a boy?
To have a nursemaid haunt my every step?

(*He leaves. The* WATER-NYMPHS *rise from the river.*)

WATER-NYMPHS
                        Sisters, shall we now pursue them,   90
                        Splashing down the open field?
                        Laughing, whistling, let's undo them,
                        Make their frightened horses yield.

                        No, too late. The dark is growing,
                        Cold the deep and colder yet,   95

Hear, the village cock is crowing,
Look, the waning moon has set.

ONE WATER–NYMPH

Stay for just a few more seconds.

A SECOND WATER–NYMPH

No, it's time, it's time to sleep.
Our Tsarina calls and beckons,   100
Waiting sternly in the deep.

(*They disappear.*)

The bottom of the Dnieper.
The water-nymphs' palace

(*They sit by their* QUEEN, *spinning.*)

QUEEN OF NYMPHS
　　The sun has set. Leave off your spinning, sisters.
　　A shaft of moonlight sparkles overhead.
　　Have done. Swim up and dance beneath the stars;
　　Go play, but don't molest a soul tonight—
　　Don't dare to tickle any passerby,　　　　　　　　　5
　　Or tangle up the nets of fishermen
　　With weeds and mud, or lure a little child
　　With tales of fishes to the murky deep.

　　　　　(*The little* WATER-NYMPH *enters.*)

　　And where were you?

HER DAUGHTER　　　　　I made my way to land,
　　To Grandad there. He keeps on asking me　　　　10
　　To fetch his money from the riverbed,
　　That money that he tossed us long ago.
　　I've looked and looked, but haven't found it yet.
　　I'm not so sure I know what money is,
　　But anyway, I brought him from the deep　　　　15
　　A bunch of shiny shells, all different hues.
　　He really liked them, too.

QUEEN　　　　　　　　The crazy miser!
　　Now listen, daughter. You've a task to do;
　　You mustn't fail. A man will come tonight
　　Down to our riverbank. Keep watch for him　　　20
　　And meet him when he comes. He's close to us,
　　Your father, child.

DAUGHTER　　　　Is he the one that left?
　　The one that fled to marry someone else?

QUEEN

    The very one. But give him your affection,
    And tell him all you know about your birth,   25
    The things I've told you of, and also speak
    Of me as well. And if he wants to know,
    If I've forgotten him or not, you'll say
    That I remember him and love him still,
    And long to see him soon. You understand?   30

DAUGHTER

    I understand.

QUEEN   Then go.

(alone)

             It's seven years
Since, mad with grief, I leapt into the stream.
Oh, what a desperate, foolish girl I was!
And deep within the Dnieper I became—
A cold and terrifying water-nymph.   35
Full seven years have I, each day, made plans
And brooded on the vengeance that I crave.
And now, it seems, my time has come at last.

The Dnieper shore

PRINCE

    Some unknown power seems to draw me back—
    Unwillingly—to these unhappy shores,
    Where everything reminds me of the past,
    And speaks of those now mournful, cherished days,
    Those fair and easy days when I was young.   5
    Here once upon a time I met with love,
    A passionate and freely given love.
    How happy I was then... and how insane
    To turn away from such a priceless gift.
    What melancholy, melancholy thoughts   10
    That meeting yesterday evoked in me.
    How terrible he is, her wretched father!
    I wonder if he'll come again today?
    And if he might agree to leave his woods
    And come to live with us...   15

    (*The little* WATER-NYMPH *approaches from the riverbank.*)

                  What's this I see?
From where did you appear, my lovely child?

EXPLANATORY NOTES

BORIS GODUNOV

1 *Dedication*: Pushkin dedicated the work to Nikolai Karamzin, his friend and an eminent historian, whose *History of the Russian State* served as a major source for the characters and events of Pushkin's drama.

6 *Characters in the Play*: not listed in the original.

Scene 1

9 *Duma boyars*: the Duma was a council or assembly of nobles that the tsar consulted or not, as he wished. The boyars were members of the old Russian nobility, many of them descended from the princes who, in Russia's era of feudal disintegration, before the consolidation of power in the hands of the Prince of Muscovy, had ruled principalities of their own.

The widowed nun-Tsarina: there was a tradition that the tsar, on nearing his death, would take the vows as a monk. His widow as well would sometimes take vows as a nun, as the Tsarina Irena has done here, upon her husband Fyodor's death.

10 *Uglich*: the provincial town about 100 miles north of Moscow where the widowed last wife of Ivan IV resided with her young son, Dimitry, after her forced removal from the capital. It was there, in 1591, that the young prince suffered a mysterious and violent death.

Reveal it all to Fyodor: Fyodor, the tsar who has just died, was the son of Ivan IV, but a weak-willed figure not suited to his role as monarch. Power during his reign was already firmly in the hands of his brother-in-law, Boris Godunov, who served as regent.

11 *Malyuta*: Malyuta Skuratov, the father of Boris's wife, was a torturer and executioner under Ivan IV, an agent of his paranoid ferocities against both real and imagined enemies.

He'll grasp the crown and cape of Monomakh: the name of Monomakh is mentioned here and again in Scene 10 and in the penultimate Scene 22. The reference is to Vladimir Monomakh, the prince who ruled Kievan Russia in the early twelfth century. It was after his death in 1125 that the effort to hold the Russian principalities together in a unified state collapsed. Rulers of the later Russian state of Muscovy referred to themselves as the heirs of Monomakh and to his fur-trimmed crown as 'shapka Monomakha', the 'cap of Monomakh'.

Rurik: the half-legendary Varangian (Scandinavian) prince who in the ninth century, with his brothers Sineus and Truvor, came with a small force of Norsemen to settle on eastern Slavic, or Russian, territory. The subsequent rulers of the first Russian state, situated in Kiev, considered themselves descendants of this Rurik. Many of the boyar princes in later times also claimed descent from this line of earlier rulers and considered themselves the equals of the tsar's family.

Scene 2

13 *the Red Porch*: an ornamental landing and staircase in the Moscow Kremlin. It was destroyed in the 1930s and recently reconstructed. The Russian word for 'red' (*krasnyi*) in former times meant 'beautiful'.

Scene 3

15 *The Maidens' Field*: a large open space on what was then the outskirts of Moscow near the Novodevichy Convent, where Boris is sequestered with his sister, Tsar Fyodor's widow, as he apparently resists all efforts to have him take the crown.

Scene 4

17 *the tombs where Russia's great deceasèd rulers rest*: the tsars, and before them the Grand Princes of Muscovy, were buried in the Archangel Cathedral in the Kremlin.

Scene 5

20 *when Tatar hordes held sway*: from the mid-thirteenth century until the mid-fifteenth century, the weak and small Russian principalities collapsed under the onslaught of Mongol armies led by descendants of Genghis Khan. For two centuries the Russian city-states were vassals of the ruling Khan of the Golden Horde. Towards the end of the fourteenth century, Russian forces began a gradual reconquest of the Tatar principalities, and by the time of Ivan IV the reacquisition of their lands by the Russians was more or less complete.

stormy Novgorod and its Assembly: Novgorod had been annexed by Muscovy under Ivan III. It still retained the vestiges of a semi-independent assembly, which Ivan IV destroyed in a bloody attack on the town.

21 *the towers of Kazan*: situated on the Volga, the khanate of Kazan was one of the last strongholds of the Tatars. Ivan IV destroyed the fortifications and incorporated the khanate into Russia in 1552. The tsar then had the Chapel of St Basil's erected on Red Square to commemorate the event.

Scene 6

26 *send him off to Solovetsky*: Solovetsky was a monastery, situated in the far north, on islands near the Arctic Circle. It was a fortress and a place of banishment for religious and political offenders.

Scene 7

28 *I sought my daughter's happiness in marriage*: Boris had intended to marry his daughter Ksenia to Prince John of Denmark, brother of the Danish

king, but the young man died in 1602, shortly after he arrived in Russia and before the marriage could take place.

Scene 8

29 *the Polish border*: Poland at the time was part of a joint Kingdom of Poland and Lithuania. Pushkin refers to this hostile neighbour of Russia as either Poland or Lithuania. For the sake of consistency and clarity I have referred to the country only as Poland.

Scene 9

37 *PUSHKIN*: Afanasy Pushkin is an invented character, a composite of several actual Pushkins who opposed Boris. The Gavrila Pushkin who appears later in the drama is a real ancestor of the poet.

crown prince: here the term refers to Ivan's son Dimitry. The title of the Russian monarch is tsar (the word derives from 'Caesar'); and the term for the tsar's son and heir is tsarevich. I have translated the latter word sometimes as 'Crown Prince' and at other times have retained the term 'tsarevich'.

38 *Sigismund the King*: Sigismund III, King of Poland (1587–1632), who spent much of his reign in a struggle with Russia to dominate Eastern Europe.

39 *the great Romanov princes*: Pushkin's mild tribute to the dynasty that ruled Russia in his own time.

he binds the serfs in place forever: under Boris Godunov, in 1601, the peasants' right to transfer from one estate to another (at the end of the harvest or on St George's Day in November) was abolished, which marked the beginning of serfdom in Russia.

Scene 10

42 *Cracow*: traditional residence of the Polish kings.

Scene 11

48 *Peter's vicar*: the clergy of Catholic Poland had hopes, in the event of the conquest of Russia, of converting the country from Eastern Orthodoxy to the Latin Church. Kievan Russia had officially adopted Orthodox Christianity from the Byzantine Empire in 998.

St Ignatius: founder of the Jesuit Order, which sought to further the spread of Roman Catholicism throughout the world.

49 *Kurbsky*: a fictional son of the Prince Andrei Kurbsky who was at one time a favourite of Ivan IV (he had aided the tsar in the conquest of the khanate of Kazan). He later fell out of favour with the tsar and became his vociferous adversary. Forced to flee for his life, he defected to Poland and spent the rest of his life in exile.

50 *Volhynian lands*: Volhynia, a region in south-western Ukraine, then belonging to Poland.

King Stefan: Stefan Bathory, King of Poland (1575–86), and his successor, Sigismund III, both attempted to conquer Russia. Bathory stopped Ivan IV in his attempt to acquire access to the Baltic and forced him to cede territory to both Poland and Sweden. Andrei Kurbsky had become a supporter of the Polish king in his war against Ivan IV.

51 *hetmen*: (or *ataman*): a chief of the semi-nomadic and semi-independent bands that inhabited the southern parts of European Russia. Large communities of these people, mostly peasants, had fled Muscovy in order to escape serfdom and avoid heavy taxation. They settled along the Don and Dnieper rivers.

52 *Musa gloriam coronat, gloriaque musam*: 'The muse crowns glory, and glory crowns the muse.'

Scene 16

70 Margeret and Rosen, actual historical figures, were foreign officers in the tsar's service. A rough translation of their macaronic expostulations on the cowardice of the Russian troops under their command follows:

M   What does this word 'Orsòdox' mean?... These cursèd riff-raff, rotten scum! Devil take it, sir, I'm damned enraged; you'd think they have no arms to fight with, only legs to run with.

R   It's a disgrace.

M   A plague on them! I'll not retreat a step—once the wine is poured, you drink it (that is, once a thing is started, you finish it). What do you say to that, sir?

R   You're quite right.

M   Damn me, the fighting's getting hot! That devil—that Pretendair as they call him—that rascal has some real hair on his ass... What do you think, sir?

R   Oh, yes!

M   Look there... look! There's action against the enemy's rear guard. It must be our valiant Basmanoff making an assault; good for him!

R   I think it is.

M   And here come our Germans! Gentlemen!... Order them, sir, to form up and, damn it, we'll attack!

·R   Excellent. Form up, men! March!

THE GERMANS   With God's help!

Scene 20

81 *So thought Ivan the Third*: Ivan III, sometimes called 'the Great', was the grandfather of Ivan IV (the Dread). During his reign as Grand

Prince (1462–1505) he greatly enlarged the territory of Muscovy. He annexed the Republic of Novgorod and other Russian principalities and in effect created a unified state under the leadership of Moscow. He was the first Russian ruler to assume the title 'tsar'.

84 *the vestment... and the holy vows*: the tsar, in medieval times, by tradition took the vows of a monk on his deathbed.

Scene 22

89 *The Place of Proclamations*: a raised platform on Red Square where the tsar's edicts were read to the people. The area is also sometimes called 'the Place of Executions', since beheadings often took place nearby.

A SCENE FROM FAUST

Written in 1826, this brief dramatic dialogue is an original composition and not a translation from Goethe's *Faust*. Because of its extreme brevity and its use of the rhymed iambic tetrameter that was one of Pushkin's favourite metres (used notably in his verse novel, *Eugene Onegin*), it has often been classed as a lyrical rather than a dramatic work. The piece may also be viewed, however, as a precursor of *The Little Tragedies*, which were first planned by Pushkin at about the same time, although they would not be completed until some four years later.

THE LITTLE TRAGEDIES

Each of these four short plays, unlike most of Pushkin's other works, has a foreign setting, and each takes place in a different Western European country and in a historical period far removed from Pushkin's own day.

THE MISERLY KNIGHT

Pushkin's claim that his drama is based on scenes from a tragicomedy by the English poet William Shenstone (1714–63) is a bit of obfuscation on his part. There is no such play by Shenstone, and Pushkin's fabrication is partly explained by his wish to disguise certain autobiographical elements in the work: the poet's own father was notoriously stingy with his son and their relations were strained.

MOZART AND SALIERI

Pushkin uses as a basis for his play the rumour, widespread in Austria in the late 1820s, that the Italian composer Antonio Salieri (1750–1825), on his deathbed, confessed to having poisoned Mozart.

Scene 1

124 *Gluck*: the German opera composer Christoph Willibald Gluck

(1714–87), who revolutionized opera with a new unity of drama, music, and emotion.

124 *Piccinni*: the Italian opera composer Niccolò Piccinni (1728–1800), whose works were popular all over Europe and who served as a champion for those who favoured the Italian operatic tradition over the new, more realistic style advanced by Gluck.

Iphigenia: an opera by Gluck.

125 *Voi che sapete*: ('You who know'), an aria from Mozart's opera, *The Marriage of Figaro*.

Scene 2

130 *Tarare*: Salieri's opera based on a text by the French dramatist Pierre Beaumarchais (1732–99).

THE STONE GUEST

The drama's epigraph ('O most illustrious statue of the great Commander! Ah, master!') is taken from Lorenzo Da Ponte's Italian libretto of Mozart's opera, *Don Giovanni*.

A FEAST IN TIME OF PLAGUE

Pushkin's short drama is more an adaptation than a translation; it is based on a scene in Act 1 of *The City of the Plague*, a play by the Scottish writer, John Wilson (1789–1854). The songs of Mary and the Master of Revels, the only passages in *The Little Tragedies* that are rhymed, are essentially Pushkin's own.

Pushkin's interest in the theme of Wilson's tragedy was stimulated by the outbreak of cholera that detained him at his estate of Boldino in the autumn of 1830.

American Literature

British and Irish Literature

Children's Literature

Classics and Ancient Literature

Colonial Literature

Eastern Literature

European Literature

Gothic Literature

History

Medieval Literature

Oxford English Drama

Poetry

Philosophy

Politics

Religion

The Oxford Shakespeare

A complete list of Oxford World's Classics, including Authors in Context, Oxford English Drama, and the Oxford Shakespeare, is available in the UK from the Marketing Services Department, Oxford University Press, Great Clarendon Street, Oxford OX2 6DP, or visit the website at www.oup.com/uk/worldsclassics.

In the USA, visit www.oup.com/us/owc for a complete title list.

Oxford World's Classics are available from all good bookshops. In case of difficulty, customers in the UK should contact Oxford University Press Bookshop, 116 High Street, Oxford OX1 4BR.